AI BOOKS (continued)

Jackson *Introduction to Expert Systems*

Kandel *Fuzzy Mathematical Techniques with Applications*

Kearsley (Ed.) *Artificial Intelligence and Instruction: Applications and Methods*

Klahr & Waterman (Eds.) *Expert Systems: Techniques, Tools and Applications*

Manna & Waldinger *The Logical Basis for Computer Programming.* Volume 1: *Deductive Reasoning*

Marcus *Prolog Programming: Applications for Database Systems, Expert Systems and Natural Language Systems*

Pearl *Heuristics: Intelligent Search Strategies for Computer Problem Solving*

Rogers *A Prolog Primer*

Rogers *A Turbo Prolog Primer*

Sager *Natural Language Information Processing: A Computer Grammar of English and its Applications*

Sager, Friedman & Lyman *Medical Language Processing: Computer Management of Narrative Data*

Silverman (Ed.) *Expert Systems for Business*

Sowa *Conceptual Structures: Information Processing in Mind and Machine*

Walker (Ed.), McCord, Sowa & Wilson *Knowledge Systems and Prolog: A Logical Approach to Expert Systems and Natural Language Processing*

Waterman *A Guide to Expert Systems*

Wilensky *Planning and Understanding: A Computational Approach to Human Reasoning*

Winograd *Language as a Cognitive Process.* Volume 1: *Syntax*

Winston *Artificial Intelligence*, 2nd Edition

Winston & Horn *LISP*, 2nd Edition

Structured Induction in Expert Systems

Turing Institute Press

The Turing Institute, located in Glasgow, Scotland, was established in 1983 as a not-for-profit company, named in honour of the late Alan M. Turing, the distinguished British mathematician and logician whose work has had a lasting influence on the foundations of modern computing.

The Institute offers integrated research and teaching programmes in advanced intelligent technologies – in particular, logic programming, computer vision, robotics and expert systems. It derives its income from research and training contracts, both governmental and industrial, and by subscription from its Industrial Affiliates. It assists Affiliates with the transfer of technology from research to application, and provides them with training for their technical staff, a wide range of software tools, and a comprehensive library and information service.

The Turing Institute is an Academic Associate of the University of Strathclyde, and its research staff work closely with different departments of the University on a variety of research programmes.

Other titles published in association with the Turing Institute Press

Applications of Expert Systems
J. Ross Quinlan (Editor)

Knowledge-Based Programming
Enn Tyugu

Structured Induction in Expert Systems

Alen D. Shapiro
Cogensys Corporation (formerly at the Turing Institute)

TURING INSTITUTE PRESS
in association with

ADDISON-WESLEY PUBLISHING COMPANY
Wokingham, England · Reading, Massachusetts
Menlo Park, California · New York · Don Mills, Ontario
Amsterdam · Bonn · Sydney · Singapore · Tokyo
Madrid · Bogota · Santiago · San Juan

The programs in this book have been included for their instructional value. They have been tested with care but are not guaranteed for any particular purpose. The publisher does not offer any warranties or representations, nor does it accept any liabilities with respect to the programs.

Cover design by Crayon Design, Henley-on-Thames.
Typeset by Columns, Reading.
Printed in Great Britain by The Bath Press, Avon.
First printed 1987

British Library Cataloguing in Publication Data
Shapiro, Alen D.
Structured induction in expert systems.
(Turing Institute Press).
1. Expert systems (Computer science)
I. Title II. Turing Institute
006.3′3 QA76.76.E95

ISBN 0–201–17813–3

Library of Congress Cataloging-in-Publication Data
Shapiro, Alen D., 1956–
Structured induction in expert systems.
(The Turing Institute Press)
Bibliography: p.
Includes index.
1. Expert systems (Computer science) 2. Electronic data processing – Structured techniques. I. Title.
II. Series: Turing Institute Press (Series)
QA76.76.E95S49 1987 006.3′3 87–14404

ISBN 0–201–17813–3 (Addison-Wesley)

This book is dedicated to my wife Merryl who has stood by me through thick and thin, triumph and defeat, keeping me sane and showing me the meaning of love. Also to my parents Rene and Harvey for whose confidence and support I will always be grateful.

Preface

This book is a detailed report of an experiment to determine if machine learning may be used to alleviate the 'expert system bottleneck' (Feigenbaum, 1977). In order to ensure measurability of the results, restricted, yet surprisingly complex, chess endgames were used as an 'experimental test-bench'. Although this is not a book about chess, a level of detail consistent with an experimental report was necessary, specifically in Chapters 3, 6 and 7. A good insight into the complexity of the tasks attempted may be gained by reading these chapters; however, since most necessary information from these chapters is cross-referenced in the text, the casual reader need not feel over-burdened.

The book is aimed at a wide variety of readers and the techniques described have been implemented in commercial rule induction systems which have been successfully applied to 'real-world' problems. The layout of the book is as follows:

Chapter 1 states the problem to be solved, gives a brief history of computer induction and sets the scene for the use of chess as an experimental test-bench.

Chapter 2 describes the programming tools used, namely ID3, Interactive ID3, CLIP/C, decision-vector generators and database generators. The chapter starts with a definition of the chess notation used throughout the rest of the book. Chapter 3 describes the need for, and process of, database generation for result-checking purposes.

Chapter 4 describes how computer induction was leashed in order that it might produce usable products. The techniques of 'structured induction' and 'self-commenting' (including post-processing of self-commentary text) are described. Chapter 5 is an overview of the two experiments performed and their aims.

Chapter 6 describes in detail the three-piece (KPK) endgame solution that was generated. The latter portion of this chapter is given to comparing the cost of generating this structured solution (as a program manufacturing task) with more conventional solutions (unstructured induction and database lookup).

Chapter 7 contains a detailed description of the four-piece (KPa7KR) endgame solution that was generated. The latter portion of this chapter is a report on how structured and unstructured solutions were compared, their run-time efficiency and accuracy.

Chapter 8 is the most important chapter of the book. It contains a general discussion on: a) the effectiveness of computer induction; b) where 'rules of thumb' might fit in; c) if a domain-expert exists, the unsuitability of unstructured induction; d) the measured information content associated with the expert-supplied structure; e) human understandability of machine-generated rules (criteria that would allow such a rule-set, when run, to be called an expert system); f) the nature of rule languages that would only code human-compatible rules (machine-generated or otherwise); and g) the conclusions drawn from this work.

Acknowledgements

Part of the work described in this book was done while the author was in receipt of an SRC Studentship in association with a project funded by SRC grant no. GR/A/80327 made to Professor Donald Michie for software and microelectronic aids for design and implementation of expert systems. The author acknowledges provision of facilities from the University of Edinburgh, Intelligent Terminals Ltd, the Turing Institute and Citicorp/TTI and expresses his thanks to Professor Donald Michie for his encouragement and helpful suggestions in particular as regards the treatment of information measurement followed in Section 8.4. The author also wishes to express his thanks to Dr Timothy Niblett for his help and for the provision of the KPK and KPKR databases and to Ken Thompson for providing the KQKR and KRKR databases. Thanks also to former Scottish Chess Champion Danny Kopec for acting as an expert in providing examples for the KPKR domain and to Rob Gordon and Marcel Schoppers for their invaluable help with the early stages of KPKR. The author also acknowledges financial assistance from International Computers Ltd and the General Electric Company.

Part of Chapter 6 has appeared in *Advances in Computer Chess 3* (Ed. M. R. B. Clarke) Shapiro and Niblett (1982). Most of the work described in this book was submitted in partial requirement for the degree of Ph.D. in Machine Intelligence (Shapiro, 1983). Part of Chapter 4 has appeared in *Advances in Computer Chess 4* (Ed. D. F. Beal) Shapiro and Michie (1986).

The author and publishers would like to thank the *IBM Journal of Research and Development* for permission to reproduce an extract from A. Newell, J. C. Shaw and H. A. Simon's 'Chess-playing programs and the problem of complexity', *IBM J. Res. Dev.* **2**, 320–335. Copyright 1958 by International Business Machines Corporation; reprinted with permission.

Contents

Chapter 1

Introduction

1.1 Motivation

An 'expert system' is a computer program that aims to:

1. emulate or outdo one or more human experts in a skilled diagnostic or other decision-making task; and
2. explain its decisions to the user on demand.

The structure of an expert system can be split into three modules:

- the **inference engine**;
- the **knowledge-base**; and
- the **knowledge acquisition module**.

The knowledge-base contains a representation of expertise in the domain. There is also a **'database'** which contains transient information specific to the current state of the problem. The inference engine dictates how the rules in the knowledge-base are applied to the facts present from time to time in the 'database'. Database is placed in quotation marks because, firstly, this usage is misleading – 'situation model' would perhaps be better – and, secondly, 'database' is used later for something different. Use of the knowledge acquisition module usually requires a partnership between a computer scientist (knowledge engineer) and a specialist (domain expert) in the given field. Sometimes these are one and the same person.

To make an expert system one must choose (or develop) an inference engine and, consulting a domain expert, fill the knowledge-base with information of a type which can be called 'prescriptive'. This typically has the form of 'if–then' rules, each with associated degrees of confidence. For example, *if* (with some degree of certainty) the car battery is flat *then* conclude (with some measure of confidence) that the fan belt is loose. Some expert domains are such that a system with all confidence measures set to 0 or 1 (false or true) is adequate.

The choice of inference engine dictates the user–interface characteristics and defines some ordering over the information contained in the knowledge-base. Designing an inference engine is now well understood. At first glance, knowledge gathering from the domain expert may also not seem to be particularly hard. But it has become increasingly apparent that:

> 'the acquisition of domain knowledge [is] the bottleneck problem in the building of applications-oriented intelligent agents'. (Feigenbaum, 1977)

Even with domain experts who are regularly available (by no means the normal situation since by their nature their time is in heavy demand) one rule per man-day debugged and installed in the knowledge-base is reckoned adequate progress.

What is so difficult about getting correct rules out of an expert, since he is after all an expert? To answer this question it is important to realize that his expertise does not include the ability to explain the reasons for his professional decisions. When a chemical company hires a mass spectroscopist it is renting his ability to *interpret* spectra, not to explain how he makes the interpretations. Hence he is not to be regarded as necessarily expert in this second activity. Indeed in this activity he is not even in the normal sense a professional. Experts typically cannot describe their own reasoning processes. They have to a large extent forgotten how they learned their trade, which tends to be largely based on experience assimilated into a form of intuitive 'know-how'. Moreover, domain experts are seldom computer scientists; hence they do not know how to install rules in a given software system nor do they know the form the rules should take for a particular inference engine. A direct interface between domain expert and expert system is needed. At present the interface is via the knowledge engineer. The knowledge engineer talks to the expert and extracts rules from the explanations he supplies, converting them to machine-acceptable form and pointing out inconsistencies as they are discovered. This is the long, slow process of rule acquisition referred to before. The indications of the present work are that for moderately complex tasks complete success can never be achieved by this method alone, i.e. without use of rule induction. It is significant that the largest operational rule-bases to be built without using induction have not yet much exceeded 2000 rules. Nievergelt (1977) showed that a grand-master's store of chess patterns amounts to some 50 000 in number. Although one pattern is not always equivalent to one rule, the implications for the construction of expert systems for problems of grand-master chess complexity are clear.

However, there is one facet of the expert's skill that until recently has not been utilized: he is able to act as a skilled source of relevant examples to train an apprentice. If this skill could be tapped and fed into an expert system equipped with the power to generalize from examples it should alleviate the knowledge-gathering bottleneck. Michalski and Chilausky (1980) have shown that it is possible by the use of mechanized inductive learning to build a complete expert system from a file of examples. Moreover, the inductively built expert system was not only much cheaper to synthesize than a comparable system hand-built by conventional techniques but also showed strikingly superior accuracy of run-time decisions. The research, which was on diagnosing diseases in soy beans, showed that, at this level of problem complexity, the induced rules were understandable and mentally checkable by human experts in the test domain. These issues of cognitive compatibility are central and are more fully discussed in Section 1.6.

Another feature usually associated with expert systems is that of 'knowledge refinement'. The information content of an active knowledge-base tends to increase as it is tuned and rules are added. It becomes an increasingly accurate store of expert chosen rules that with very little reformatting can be turned into a tutorial manual.

1.2 Historical background

The following selection from published contributions on machine learning over the past 25 years is focused on just those which point to the possibility of incorporating learning in expert systems software. We omit work like that of Samuel (1957) based on the tuning of parameters of a pre-specified description as opposed to the structural modification of descriptions or the generation of new descriptions.

Hunt *et al.*'s (1966) CLS (Concept Learning System) was the first to generate rules automatically from examples. These generalizations were produced in the form of decision trees, functionally equivalent to compound conditional statements.

Michie and Chambers' (1968, 1969) real-time system BOXES 'learned' to balance a pole on a moving cart. The system modified a set of 225 production rules on the basis of trial runs with a simulation displayed on a video monitor. The system could acquire expertise either in stand-alone mode from its own trial and error, or by observing the real-time decisions of an expert trained on the control task.

Winston (1970) and Barrow and Popplestone (1971) independently introduced relational graphs ('semantic nets') to describe visual scenes. Their programs modified these visual descriptions from example scenes.

Michalski, together with Chilausky and Jacobsen (Chilausky *et al.*, 1976), showed cost-benefit advantages, both in the labour of rule-base construction and in run-time performance, of induction over traditional dialogue methods for building an expert rule-base. Michalski later (1980) took his soy bean diagnosis a stage further with new material and multiple sources of expert knowledge for a more detailed comparison. The induced expert system again outperformed an expert system generated by conventional means of rule acquisition from plant pathologists. User transparency of machine rules was reasonable, although not ideal.

Quinlan (1979) redesigned CLS on a more rational and efficient basis and adapted it to large example files by introducing a 'refutation filter'. The latter incrementally adds a selection of counter-examples to the working set, re-inducing an improved rule on each iteration. A full description of this algorithm is given later.

Quinlan (1983) produced machine-executable descriptions with five times greater run-time efficiency than the best human-produced descriptions. He also (1983) proved bounds on the run-time error of induced descriptions to be small and a function *only* of the size of training set.

1.3 Nature of reasoning

Two forms of logical reasoning are normally distinguished under the names **deductive** and **inductive**. Deductive reasoning is the process of reasoning from the general to the particular. The first recorded attempt at formalizing deduction was Aristotle's (see for example his *Analytica Posteriora* translated in McKeon, 1947). Following deductive rules one may deduce:

- facts from theories, e.g. determine whether a particular bridge will stand by axiomatizing and applying the laws of mechanics (an example of Aristotle's own is to determine whether a particular triangle has angles summing to two right angles by applying the laws of geometry);
- more specific theories from less specific theories, e.g. to classify a class of bridges (or triangles) as capable of standing (or satisfying the two right angles condition, e.g. the class of plane triangles).

Rules for inductive reasoning were given by Francis Bacon in his *Novum Organum*. Induction is in a sense the reverse of deduction, i.e. reasoning from the particular to the general. Following its rules one may induce:

- theories from facts, e.g. in 'scientific induction'. Thus Galileo was able to develop theories of motion from observing metal spheres rolling down inclined planes. Similarly, legal codifiers abstract over empirical accumulations of judicial precedents;
- more general from less general theories, as when Newton's scheme subsumed the partial formulations of Kepler concerning planetary motions.

Deduction guarantees that providing the theories used are correct, the deduced facts and more specific theories are also correct. Induction is a type of informed conjecture and no equivalent statement can be made, except in the special case that the training set of examples exhausts the entire universe of instances. Here the use of an induced theory is as a compact replacement for the facts rather than as a predictor of new facts. Thus induced descriptions are guaranteed valid only for the facts and sub-descriptions from which the induction was made. When a fact or class of facts is encountered which is misclassified by the description (a refutation example), a further cycle of induction is entered to construct or reconstruct a new description which fits the enlarged set of examples. Essential to the inductive cycle is the availability, at every stage, of a source of information as to whether each given example does or does not satisfy the current descriptive role. We call such a source an 'oracle'. An oracle may be a tutor, or it may be (as in 'scientific induction') the response of the real world to observation or experiment. Finally it may be a 'fossil record' inscribed in machine memory by some exhaustive computation. This last form of oracle, important in the present work, is commonly (if misleadingly) referred to by the name 'database'.

The reason that it is not in general possible to provide an inverse to the deduction function is that unless *all* relevant facts are available, a collection of facts is not a replacement for a theory and a theory induced from an incomplete set of facts may always be refuted when further facts come to light. However, the process of generating theories from possibly incomplete example sets is one of the mechanisms by which human concept learning takes place. When it is performed by machine the process is called **inductive inference** or **computer induction**.

1.4 The products of induction: friendly *versus* unfriendly

Human understandability is a key facet of expert system design. If a human professional cannot question and follow the reasoning processes of an automated system he cannot be expected to endorse its decisions and he will not use it even if he knows that statistically it may outperform him. If he does use it then he runs the risk of overriding its decisions at the wrong time through his lack of understanding of the machine's 'game plan'. Kopec (1982) illustrates this point with the following example.

In 1975 the productivity of the Hoogovens hot strip mill dropped abruptly and the question was, to what extent was this problem caused by a newly installed highly automated control system. Reporting on an 18-month study Voysey (1977) stated that the operators failed to understand fully the control theory of the programs used in the controlling computer, and this reinforced their attitude of 'standing well back' from the operation – except when things were very clearly going awry. By intervening late, the operators let the productivity drop below that of plants using traditional control methods. So automation had led to lower productivity and operator alienation simultaneously.

Among the recommendations of the enquiry was the following:

> '*Information displays should be designed to help the operator predict performance and to help him* understand *the decisions being taken by the automation, as opposed to the use of displays only to indicate the state of a process.*'

In this case the result was not too disastrous. However, if the task environment were an air traffic control centre or nuclear power station mistakes like those illustrated above could then cost lives. On the other hand lives might be lost if advanced automation were *not* used.

One answer to this dilemma is not to make 'unfriendly' man–machine systems in the first place. But it is already plain that the cost-effective production of expert systems themselves is a task that due to problem complexity needs to be performed (at least in part) by computer induction. This tool will then need to be constrained to produce only human-friendly (understandable) rules. This book reports a technique, structured induction, which enables this to be done.

1.5 Choice of chess as experimental test-bench

Newell *et al.* (1958) in their paper 'Chess-playing programs and the problem of complexity' justified interest in chess from the artificial intelligence viewpoint in the following way:

> '*Chess is the intellectual game* par excellence. *Without a chance device to obscure the contest, it pits two intellects against each other in a situation so complex that neither can hope to understand it completely, but sufficiently amenable to analysis that each can hope to out-think his opponent. The game is sufficiently deep and subtle in its implications to have supported the rise of professional players, and to have allowed a deepening analysis through 200 years of intensive study and play without becoming exhausted or barren. Such characteristics mark chess as a natural area for attempts at mechanization. If one could devise a successful chess machine, one would seem to have penetrated to the core of human intellectual endeavour.*'

Michie (1982) identifies five key features that together make chess specially interesting when it comes to the study of the representation of human knowledge in machines.

1. The game constitutes a fully defined and well-formalized domain.

2. The game challenges the highest levels of human intellectual capacity.
3. The challenge extends over a large range of cognitive functions such as logical calculation, rote learning, concept formation, analogical thinking, imagination, deductive and inductive reasoning.
4. A massive and detailed corpus of knowledge has been accumulated.
5. A generally accepted numerical scale of performance is available.

Other problem domains exhibit some of the above features, all of which are important if quantitative scientific analysis is to be performed on a non-trivial, human-taxing task. Figure 1.1 puts some other 'hard' tasks in this perspective.

Feature \ Task	School algebra	Travelling salesman	Preparing abstracts	Analytical chemistry	IQ tests	Chess
Fully defined well-formalized domain	yes	yes	no	no	no	yes
Challenges human intellectual capacity	no	yes	no	yes	yes	yes
Challenge across large range of cognitive functions	no	no	yes	no	?	yes
Massive knowledge corpus available	no	no	no	yes	no	yes
Numerical performance scale available	no	yes	no	no	yes	yes

Figure 1.1 Chess: a useful test domain. Some candidate tasks tabulated against features that would facilitate their use as test-bed problem domains. Note that only chess scores 'yes' for *all* criteria. The symbol '?' indicates that the matter is controversial.

Chess is so complex a test-bed that it would be unsuitable as a tool for measuring the success or failure of current inductive learning techniques were it not for the fact that by simple removal of pieces the problem may be reduced to less complex subproblems. In the experiments detailed later, all but three or four pieces were removed to reduce problem complexity to tractable limits. At the three-piece level (king and pawn against king) conventionally generated (human written) programs already existed that could assign a game value to any position in the problem space. There was also available a complete database of position values that could be used as an oracle. Not all these programs were 100% accurate (as the database showed). The programming problem was thus hard though not insoluble. At the four-piece level (king and pawn against king and rook) the problem is thought to be too complex to be solved by conventional programming techniques short of complete enumeration of the space of positions. Such enumerations were performed in the present work to generate exhaustive lookup databases for reference and checking purposes.

1.6 The hypothesis to be tested

The expert tasks selected were, firstly, the classification of the king and pawn versus king ending (KPK, 83 622 legal positions with Black to move) into the classes 'won' and 'drawn'; and, secondly, the classification of a chess ending comprising 209 718 legal positions into the decision classes 'won' and 'not-won' for White, the ending in question being king and pawn (the pawn situated on a7) against king and rook, with White to move (KPa7KR with WTM).

A question common to both tasks was:

> *For these domains is it possible to construct a complete and brain-compatible symbolic representation of the expert classificatory skill?*

By 'brain compatible' we mean that a person can understand the representation and can also check it by mental application to any given example case. Note that some of today's computer programs fail the first criterion and almost all fail the second.

For the more complex domain (KPa7KR) it was known that

1. no such representation had ever been constructed by human agency;
2. since the expertise is largely inaccessible to conscious review, no such representations, in the opinion of the chess masters consulted, could ever be so constructed;
3. no representations (brain compatible or otherwise) could be

constructed by known programming techniques other than by exhaustion of the domain;

4. because of the inaccessibility of expertise to conscious review (2 above) the so-called 'knowledge engineering' techniques of contemporary expert systems work would not be applicable;
5. in the absence of information about the structural features that automatically generated rules should exhibit, conventional use of inductive learning techniques would be inadequate. Rules generated in this way might well be complete but not brain compatible.

The last point concerns the need for constraints to be developed that will keep the products of induction within the bounds of brain compatibility. The foregoing question can now be specialized as follows:

> *Can techniques for the use of induction be developed which, for the complex domain of KPa7KR WTM, make possible the generation of a complete and correct rule of solution which is both machine executable and brain compatible. When translated into English text can such a rule constitute a training aid?*

It should be pointed out that the KPK problem, although almost trivial to a master, is too complex for any but the most scrappy and vague rules to have been articulated in existing chess manuals. For the KPa7KR problem the author is not aware that any human codification has been achieved at all. A semi-automated means for codifying skills too complex for human articulation would plainly be of wide utility.

In the event a method was developed for hand-crafting hierarchical structures for the given problem domains. This was found to supply the needed framework for successful use of computer induction to meet the criteria italicized above.

Chapter 2

Programming Tools

2.1 Conventions used

Throughout this book reference will be made to certain chess endgames and chess positions. The notation used to denote an endgame will specify white pieces in descending order of importance followed by the black counterparts (also in descending order of importance). Thus KPKR stands for the four-piece endgame with White possessing king and a pawn against Black's king and rook.

All references to chess positions will be made in algebraic form with files 'A' to 'H' from left to right along the bottom of the board and ranks '1' to '8' up the side. Pieces on particular squares will be denoted by colour (B or W) then piece type from the set [K, Q, R, B, N, P] (meaning king, queen, rook, bishop, knight, pawn) separated by a colon (':') from that piece's position. Thus BR:e4 stands for black rook on file 5 rank 4. The 'wildcard' character '?' will be used to denote any value in the legal range and the square brackets '[]' will contain ranges of legal values. Thus BR:?[1–4] stands for black rook on any file and on ranks 1 to 4 inclusive. The symbol –› when encountered between a piece name X and square Y means 'piece X moves to square Y', e.g. WK–›a4 means the white king moves to a4.

The abbreviations BTM, WTM, WFW and WFB stand for Black-to-move, White-to-move, won-for-White and won-for-Black respectively.

To designate complete endgames we reserve the freedom to drop brackets, colons, etc. where this introduces no ambiguity. Thus KPa7KR stands for WK:??WP:a7BK:??BR:??.

2.2 Computing and programming environment

A major consideration before embarking on any substantial programming effort is the facility afforded by the available computing environments. For computer-bound tasks such as chess database generation a powerful processor is a prerequisite. For software development a versatile operating system is essential. The former need was filled by the Edinburgh DEC 10 (KL10) supported by SERC's Interactive Computing

Facility. The latter need was filled by the UNIX operating system running at first on a six-user PDP 11/34 and later on an eight-user PDP 11/24. These machines were made available to the MIRU by Intelligent Terminals Limited. UNIX facilities like inter-process communication and makefile hierarchies were heavily utilized. The former was used for communicating between the inductive learning system (written in Pascal) and example transformation programs incorporating a CLIP emulator (written in C). The latter was used automatically to ensure that the executable portion of the software was always up to date with respect to the programs and data that described it.

2.3 ID3 induction program

ID3 (Iterative Dichotomizer Three), developed by Quinlan (1979), has at its heart an algorithm based on Hunt's Concept Learning System (CLS) (1966) which, given a set of situations each described in terms of features (Quinlan calls these features **attributes**) and a class value, induces a situation classification rule (providing the set of classified situations contain no 'clashes', see later). In principle, this rule is a program which can be run to determine the class values for a set of input situations. If the rule is generated from an exhaustive set of pre-classified situations it is guaranteed to classify correctly *all* legal input situations. A classified situation is represented by a sequence of attribute values together with the corresponding class value and is known as a **decision-vector**.

An extension to this algorithm made by Quinlan in ID3 enables the CLS iteratively to grow a small example set from an exhaustive file of pre-classified situations thereby allowing it to induce rules incrementally. This **working example set**, introduced by Quinlan, is made up of those examples used to induce a rule at any one stage of the inductive process. Quinlan calls this set the **window**. A brief outline of the ID3 algorithm is given in Figure 2.1.

The name of the attribute description file (mentioned earlier) is supplied as an argument to the ID3 program. The first line of this file contains the number of attributes to be used for the current induction run. Then for each attribute there is a line giving its name, number of values and symbol to be used in the decision rule for each value. Then there is a line containing the number of class values followed by a line containing the names of these class values to be used in the generated decision rule. For example, given the attribute description file shown in Figure 2.2 and the data shown in Figure 2.3, ID3 produces the decision rule shown in Figure 2.4. An example of how such a decision rule should be interpreted is given in Figure 2.5.

A more graphical representation for the same rule is given in Figure 2.6.

1. Read in an attribute description file (described later) that describes the attribute characteristics to be used for this run.
2. Initialize the working set with a random working example set of situations of user-determined size ('start with' parameter).
3. Induce a rule from the working set.
4. Deal with clashes.
5. Mark exceptions to the current rule that occur outside the working set.
6. If no exceptions are found goto (9).
7. Include a user-determined number of exceptions in the working set (increasing working-set size; 'increase by' parameter).
8. Print statistics for this iteration and goto (3).
9. Print rule and exit.

A **clash** is said to occur if two or more decision-vectors have the same attribute values but different class values. This corresponds to examples that are described with identical features but for which different actions are recommended. Step (4) involves marking, with a keyword 'clash' the point(s) in the incomplete rule where clashes arise. This informs the user that the current set of attributes is not adequate to classify the working set and another technique must be used here or the attribute set must be changed. A source of clashing decision-vectors is erroneous examples supplied by the expert. This aspect will be returned to.

Figure 2.1 Outline of the ID3 algorithm.

```
3
weather      3          wet     dry    blustery
sheltered    2          yes     no
soaked       2          yes     no
2
USE          DONT_USE
```

Figure 2.2 A sample ID3 attribute description file. The first line in the file (containing just a 3) indicates the number of attributes present in this problem.

When a complete and correct rule has been generated, the working set contains example situations that embody all the relevant features for a solution to the domain. Given formal (machine executable) definitions of the attributes used, this working set together with the induction system is a complete functional replacement for the decision-vector database for the domain as indeed is the induced rule. Likewise the decision-vector database is a replacement for the complete classification database. (It should be noted that none of these are replacements for any database

WEATHER	SHELTERED	SOAKED	DECISION CLASS
wet	no	no	USE
dry	—	—	DONT_USE
blustery	—	—	DONT_USE
—	yes	—	DONT_USE
—	—	yes	DONT_USE

Figure 2.3 A sample ID3 example file. Note the —, which means 'don't care', is an extension to ID3 introduced by the author. An example with sheltered = — is equivalent to two examples, one with sheltered = yes and the other with sheltered = no. When both sheltered and soaked have the value — as in example 2, then this is equivalent to 2 × 2, i.e. 4, fully specified examples.

```
weather
  blustery: DONT_USE
  dry: DONT_USE
  wet: sheltered
    no: soaked
      no: USE
      yes: DONT_USE
    yes: DONT_USE
```

Figure 2.4 A sample ID3 decision rule. This decision rule would be produced by ID3 if presented with the data given in the two previous figures.

Test the weather. If it is blustery or dry then don't use your umbrella otherwise (if the weather is wet) test whether you are sheltered. If you are then don't use your umbrella. If you are not (sheltered) then test if you are already soaked. If you are then don't use your umbrella, otherwise use it.

Figure 2.5 An English explanation for the 'umbrella' decision tree (shown in Figure 2.4).

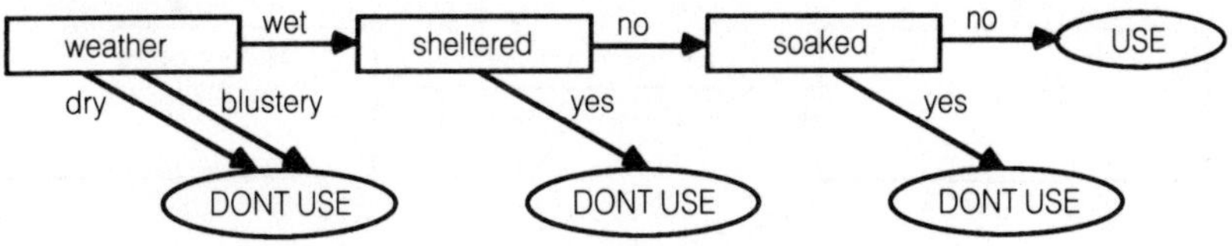

Figure 2.6 A 'nodes and arcs' representation for the same rule.

giving more information than the simple class values that appear in the decision-vectors. A rule induced from examples whose class values denote only won or not-won will not in general replace a database containing depth-of-win information.)

Resulting database compressions can be spectacular. In the case of two chess test domains (KPK and KPa7KR) the extent of this compression is shown in Figure 2.7.

Domain	Database size (space of legal positions)	Number of decision vectors classifying the total space	Size of training set required to induce a complete and correct unstructured classification rule
KPK	83 622	2412	304
KPa7KR	209 718	3196	175

Figure 2.7 KPK and KPa7KR database compression. Note that as we move from left to right in the above tabulation we traverse successive degrees of compression: from the initial universe of individuals to a smaller number of 'primitive descriptions' in the form of conjuncts of primitive descriptor values ('decision-vectors'); then from the complete set of vectors to a subset discovered by the induction algorithm as sufficient for the purpose of inducing a descriptive rule. Later we shall see that by 'structured' induction yet further compression can be achieved.

The process of database compression and the corresponding generation of a training set is shown in Figure 2.8.

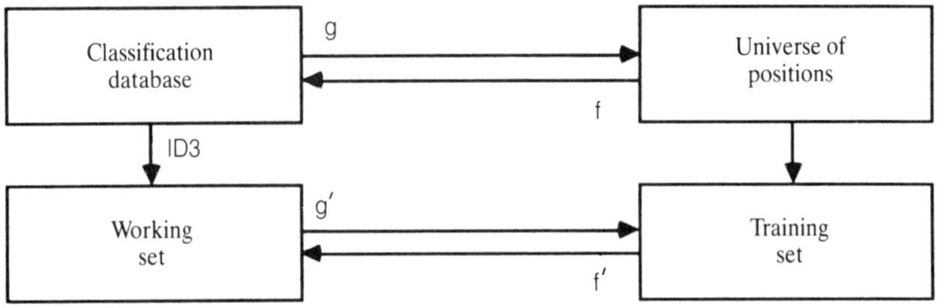

Figure 2.8 Relationship between data in ID3.

The function f, which depends on the set of attributes chosen by the domain expert, maps every chess position on to a decision-vector. Function g is chosen from the inverse f^{-1} of f (f^{-1} is not in general a function itself). The ID3 algorithm is applied to the decision-vector file producing the training set. This is a compression of the classification database in the sense that any decision rule for the training set will be a decision rule for the original file. The restriction g' of g to the working set produces a 'training set' of example positions illustrating all the features of relevance in the original universe.

2.4 Interactive ID3

Of the two problem domains to which the inductive learning technique was applied, only one (KPa7KR) was solved without using a database as oracle. In the case of KPK, since a set of databases was available, there was no problem in generating all legal decision-vectors and, by applying Quinlan's ID3, producing a complete and correct decision tree. No database was initially available, however, in the case of KPa7KR; the only source of class values was fallible human experts. In order to use Quinlan's ID3 it would have been necessary to ask these experts to supply (in advance) most if not all of the example positions (with their game values) that might be required. Experts are good at providing examples but not as a once-for-all training set supplied in advance. They function best when trying to portray single facets of the domain at a time in response to feedback from the inductive learner's mistakes. A new rule-generation tool had to be developed that allowed the interactive development of a rule by selective application of examples to a visibly developing rule. The tool was called Interactive ID3 (see Shapiro, 1983, Appendix A for a User Manual).

Interactive ID3 has been built as a shell around Quinlan's ID3 algorithm. An interactive command level allows the user to specify new examples, generate a new rule, move examples between stores ('primary' which is equivalent to Quinlan's 'window' (working set) store and 'secondary' whose use will be explained later in this section). The available commands are:

- A: add a range of examples to the primary store from the secondary store.
- C: print out the current rule as a C function. The name of this function is supplied in the attribute description file and is referred to as <prog> from here.
- D: delete a range of examples from either store.
- E: print out a range of examples in decision-vector form.

- F: read examples from the file <prog>.d.
- H or ?: print a command list help message.
- I: induce a rule from the current primary store.
- M: move a range of examples from the primary to the secondary store.
- Q: quit this program.
- R: print out the current rule as a decision tree.
- S: switch output between <prog>.out and VDU.
- T: tweak system parameters. The current set of parameters involves the format of vectors on output (E command) and the Quinlan 'start with' and 'increment by' variables.
- U: enter user's example reading routine. The user is invited to input one example and is then prompted for a class value.
- X: check the secondary store for any exceptions to the current rule. (This is done automatically after every induce command.)
- !<command>: submit <command> to the operating system for immediate execution. Interactive ID3 is suspended until this command is finished.

Examples are processed depending on their status with respect to the most recently generated decision tree. Accordingly there are four types of examples:

1. Examples that contradict the current rule.
2. Examples that do not contradict the current rule but whose decision-vectors have not been encountered before.
3. Examples that clash with examples previously encountered.
4. Examples that add no new information about the space. Their decision-vectors have been encountered before.

Examples of the first type are added immediately to the working set. Examples of the second type, though not adding any useful information at this stage, may be relevant later when the rule has changed and these examples now cause the rule to fail. This type of example is stored in the secondary store and all examples in this area are checked against subsequently generated rules. Any example in this store that fails to be classified correctly by a rule is reported to the user who has the choice as to whether it should be included in the working set. Examples of the third type are reported to the user and added to the secondary store. Examples of the fourth type are ignored.

Since it would have been impractical for the expert to supply his examples in the form of decision-vectors, Interactive ID3 was given the capability to invoke and communicate with an attribute evaluation process. In chess this means that the expert supplies his examples as board positions expressed in algebraic notation. Interactive ID3 passes the positions to an attribute evaluation process (described later) which calculates the relevant attribute values and passes them back to Interactive ID3. The expert is then prompted for a class value which is appended to the newly acquired attribute values to make a decision-vector. It is these vectors that are manipulated by Interactive ID3.

Like Quinlan's ID3, Interactive ID3 is invoked with the name of an attribute description file as its argument. In addition to the fields described in the previous section, this file has a field for a comment

```
3
weather      3      wet    dry    blustery    What's the weather like?
sheltered    2      yes    no                 Are you sheltered?
soaked       2      yes    no                 Are you already soaked?
2
USE          DONT_USE
umbrella
Should you use your umbrella?
```

Figure 2.9 A sample Interactive ID3 attribute description file.

```
#include "umbrella."

umbrella() {
  switch(weather()) {
    case BLUSTERY:
      return(DONT_USE);
    case DRY:
      return(DONT_USE);
    case WET:
      if(NOT sheltered()) {
        if(NOT soaked()) {
          return(USE);
        }
        else {
          return(DONT_USE);
        }
      }
      else {
        return(DONT_USE);
      }
  }
}
```

Figure 2.10 A C function generated by Interactive ID3.

appended to each attribute description line, a field for a question that is asked of the user as a prompt for his example class value, and a field containing the name of the relevant attribute evaluation program. This last field is also used to supply a name for the C function that may be generated. For example, recall the umbrella attribute description file. Figure 2.9 shows this file suitably changed to reflect the conventions of Interactive ID3. The same rule would be produced but now using the C command the C function shown in Figure 2.10 would be output. In this figure the first line (#include "umbrella.h") is a compiler directive to include a user-defined file in the compilation. This file must specify values for all the constants in the function. For the 'umbrella' problem the file would look as shown in Figure 2.11.

```
#define BLUSTERY      0
#define DRY           1
#define WET           2
#define USE           0
#define DONT_USE      1
#define NOT           !
```

Figure 2.11 Rule header file for the 'umbrella' problem.

Since Interactive ID3 is driven solely by the user, a technique of rule generation is needed. The best results have been obtained when the expert user is requested to select relevant examples that he thinks will be classified incorrectly by the current rule. In this way the rule is refined in a controlled and disciplined manner.

Interactive ID3 was developed for problems for which there was no classification database. But it was found useful as a tool for reducing the size of the set of examples necessary to produce a complete rule (training set). In the KPK 'canrun' example described later, the size of the training set obtained using Quinlan's ID3 with a database oracle was reduced from 16 to 12 using Interactive ID3.

2.5 CLIP/C parallel array emulator

As mentioned previously, ID3 uses situations detailed in terms of attributes. In chess these attributes can be difficult to compute though easily understandable in terms of humanly perceived patterns. Often the 'domain specialist' would express a concept that was powerful but expensive to program using conventional techniques. As with some computer vision problems, the trouble seems partly at least to arise from mismatch between the domain's intrinsically two-dimensional character and the one-dimensional architecture implicit in conventional languages. A specialized emulator was accordingly developed of an array-oriented machine for the specific purpose of coding primitive patterns. A brief description of this emulator follows. CLIP (Cellular Logic Image Processor) (Duff, 1978) is a hard-wired machine presenting the user with 32 planes of 96 × 96 bit arrays. The computations allowed are bitwise logical operations performed between planes. Since a CLIP machine was not available to us, a 100 plane 8 × 8 bit emulator was developed on the PDP 11/34. For this C-coded version, an earlier FORTRAN emulator (Zdrahal *et al.*, 1981) provided a useful design aid. The general form of a CLIP/C instruction is:

```
[c]op(plane1, plane2, plane3)
```

This means perform the logical operation op between plane1 and plane2 putting the result in plane3. The optional c in front of the operation means use the first argument complemented. Sometimes as in single-argument logical operations (e.g. not) a different number of planes is used. There are also two special functions returning Boolean values and three non-logical pattern transformation operators. The full set of library operations available with the current CLIP/C emulator is as follows:

1. Logical operations

Three-argument operations

- and(P1, P2, P3) bit-and plane P1 with plane P2 leaving the result in plane P3.
- or(P1, P2, P3) bit-or plane P1 with plane P2 leaving the result in plane P3.
- xor(P1, P2, P3) bit-xor plane P1 with plane P2 leaving the result in plane P3.
- eqv(P1, P2, P3) set all the bits in P3 that have the same value in P1 and P2.
- cand(P1, P2, P3) bit-and plane $\overline{P1}$ with plane P2 leaving the result in plane P3.
- cor(P1, P2, P3) bit-or plane $\overline{P1}$ with plane P2 leaving the result in plane P3.
- cxor(P1, P2, P3) bit-xor plane $\overline{P1}$ with plane P2 leaving the result in plane P3.
- ceqv(P1, P2, P3) bit-eqv plane $\overline{P1}$ with plane P2 leaving the result in plane P3.

Two-argument operations

- not(P1, P2) bit complement plane P1 leaving the result in plane P2.

2. Non-logical operations

Five-argument operations

- propagate(P1, P2, x, y, P3) shift bit pattern in P1 x columns in the *X* direction and y rows in the *Y* direction repeatedly until the edge of the plane is reached or an equivalent bit in plane P3 is reached. The result is left in P2. Bits falling off the edge of plane P2 are lost.

Four-argument operations

- shift(x, y, P1, P2) shift bit pattern in P1 x columns in the *X* direction and y rows in the *Y* direction leaving the result in P2. Bits falling off the edge of plane P2 are lost.

Three-argument operations

- setbit(x, y, P1) set bit (x, y) (file and rank) in plane P1. Does not affect state of any other bits in the plane.
- bitset(x, y, P1) return true if bit (x, y) is set in plane P1, otherwise false.

Two-argument operations

- expand(P1, P2) expand the bit pattern in P1 leaving the result in P2; e.g. if P1 contains 2 bits set (as below) the result would be as shown in Figure 2.12.
- copy(P1, P2) copy plane P1 leaving the result in plane P2.
- same(P1, P2) return true if plane P1 is the same as plane P2, false otherwise.

One-argument operations

- init(P1) fill plane P1 with zeros.
- zero(P1) return true if plane P1 is all zero, false otherwise.
- display(P1) print plane P1 on the console (in the same format as Figure 2.12).

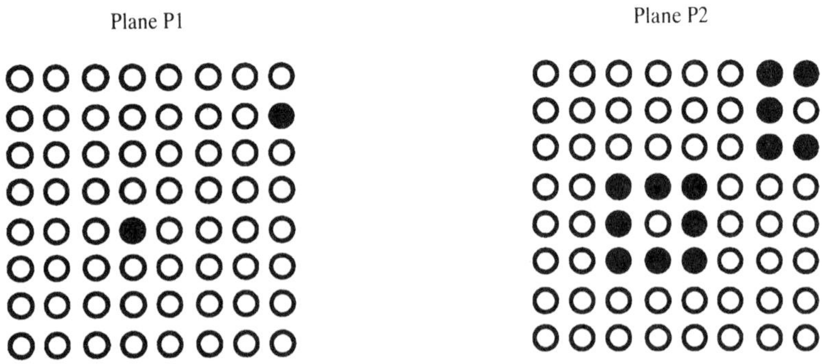

Figure 2.12 expand(P1, P2).

The speed of the CLIP/C emulator was tested on the PDP 11/34 by evaluating EXPAND, the slowest operation. One expand requires about 250 microseconds, a very acceptable time. In chess terms each bit in an 8 × 8 CLIP/C plane corresponds to a square on a chess board. If a plane containing one non-zero square is EXPANDed then the resulting CLIP/C plane represents all the squares that a king attacks from the original square.

Let BKING, WKING, PAWN, BATTACK, WATTACK and RESULT be CLIP/C planes (P1 to P6 respectively) then if the initializations shown in Figure 2.13 have been performed the CLIP/C function shown in Figure 2.14 returns the Boolean value of whether the Black king can immediately capture the pawn.

On the PDP 11/34 imcap evaluates in under 440 microseconds.

```
init(BKING);
setbit(bkfile, bkrank, BKING);
init(WKING);
setbit(wkfile, wkrank, WKING);
init(PAWN);
setbit(pfile, prank, PAWN);

expand(BKING, BATTACK);
expand(WKING, WATTACK);
```

Figure 2.13 Initializations for the imcap function.

```
imcap() {
  cand(WATTACK, BATTACK, RESULT);   /* P̅5̅.P4–›P6*/
  and(PAWN, RESULT, RESULT);   /*P3.P6–›P6*/
  return(!zero(RESULT));   /*any bits set in P6?*/
}
```

Figure 2.14 imcap – implemented using CLIP/C.

2.6 Decision-vector generators

Chess experts express their examples as chess positions. On the other hand Interactive ID3 receives its examples as decision-vectors. The conversion between these two example forms was accomplished by example transformation programs (decision-vector generators, one for each induction task). These programs comprise a loop that reads chess positions. For each legal position a series of functions is evaluated, each function corresponding to an attribute (like imcap) that the expert considers relevant to the current induction task.

In interactive mode the relevant transformation program is invoked by the inductive learning program (getting its name from the attribute description file). In non-interactive mode the relevant transformation program is compiled with (using a technique of conditional compilation) a legal move generator that generates all legal chess positions for the domain being tested. After adding the class value (from database lookup) the move generator program sorts and merges the replies to remove duplicates. The resulting decision-vector file is used as input to Quinlan's ID3.

Since the attribute transformation programs were separate UNIX processes with i/o along standard input/output channels they could be tested as separate modules independently of Interactive ID3.

2.7 Database generators

Database is used here to mean a pre-calculated collection of facts about a chess endgame. This information is ordered so that the address of any information about a position is a function of that position.

Chess databases differ from the more commonly encountered databases of facts (e.g. mathematical log tables) in one very important respect. There is generally no way to construct a particular entry in a chess database by a feasible function evaluation which does not involve reconstruction of a substantial part of the rest of the database. Exhaustive move-by-move evaluation by forward search becomes impractical at even the three-piece level. Consider the KPK endgame; about seven possible moves must be evaluated from a given position on average. To determine the value of a position by exhaustive search would require (since the maximum depth of win is 38 ply) a search tree of 7^{38} nodes. There are many ways that such a search could be speeded up (e.g. illegal and repeated move pruning) but even these methods require unacceptable resource overheads when used to evaluate a single entry in isolation.

Current chess database generation techniques require that either all of an identifiable subpart of the database be evaluated at once or none of it. This is because the developing database is used as a partial data store for other positions that may be evaluated as the algorithm progresses. Only upon completion of the algorithm is it known that data contained in the database will not be subject to further change. So until the generation process is complete no one piece of data can be said to have the correct value. Only in some cases is it possible to split the generation of a database up into parts. Furthermore, the order of evaluation of any of the subparts may be critical. For example, the generation of the KPKR WTM won-for-White/not-won-for-White database was split into six parts (one for each of the pawn ranks 2–7). Since positions with the pawn on rank 2 might lead to positions with the pawn on rank 3, the rank 3 generation had to take place before rank 2; similarly for all the other possible pawn ranks. The precise method of database generation is discussed in Chapter 3. This section is concerned with the software tools that were required to facilitate database generation.

Chess endgame databases were used in two ways:

1. provision of class values for decision-vectors in the KPK problem, i.e. using the database rather than the expert as 'oracle'; and
2. checking the accuracy of induced rules in both the KPK and KPa7KR problems.

Use of databases in the second way ensured detection of any inaccuracy of the induced product. For the KPK experiment this was confirmatory only since the same database provided class values for the vectors used to induce this rule. For the KPa7KR experiment the use of a checking database provided an invaluable cross-check since only expert-supplied information had been used to form the rule.

There were two distinct database generator programs – one for each experiment. The principles are discussed more fully in Section 3.2. In addition to these there were three intermediate databases generated in the process of creating a KPKR database for White-to-move with pawn on a7, for storing the values of 'White-wins/White-does-not-win'. (Note this KPa7KR database did not distinguish draws from Black-wins.) The problem in this case was the number of derived domains that can be encountered when either the pawn promotes or pieces are captured. These derived endgames are shown in Figure 2.15 (Px, Rx, etc. denote pawn capture, rook capture, etc.).

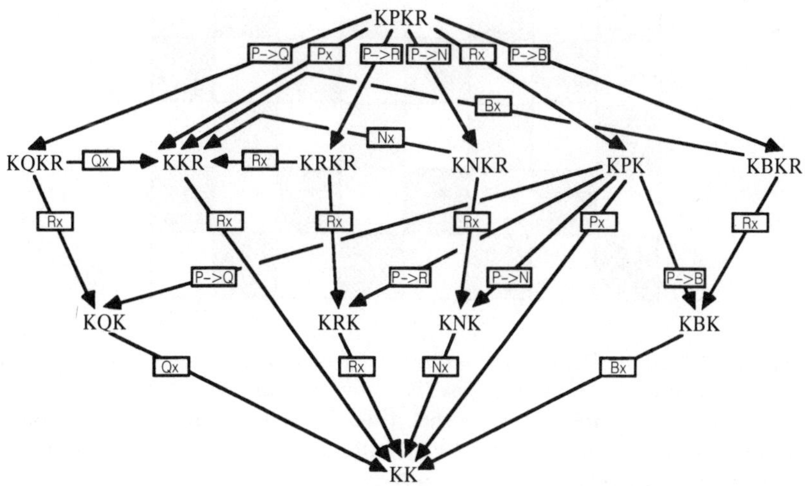

Figure 2.15 Derived endgames of KPKR.

In an attempt to cut down the work space some points were noted as follows:

1. King against king (KK) is always a draw.
2. No case where the pawn must promote to a knight is won-for-White (KNK and KNKR).
3. There are no cases when the pawn is forced to promote to a bishop (KBK and KBKR).
4. There was only one case when safe capture of the rook by the pawn could not be regarded as won-for-White (see Figure 2.16).
5. All cases where the white king captures the rook can be evaluated by the KPK subproblem rank7 (see Section 6.11).
6. Except for the position shown in Figure 2.16 (which is treated as an exception) all captures of the rook by the white pawn can be dealt with very simply.

Thus the only derived databases that it was necessary to consider when building the KPKR database were KRKR and KQKR with 'White-wins/White-does-not-win' information. These databases were kindly supplied by Ken Thompson of Bell Laboratories. Because of the nature of the database generation procedure, these databases only needed to

Figure 2.16 Can the BR be captured safely? When the WP captures the BR and promotes to either a queen or a rook the above position results in the stalemate position shown in Figure 2.17. Note that if the BR is not captured the position is won-for-Black and if, on capturing the rook, the pawn promotes to anything other than a rook or queen the position is drawn.

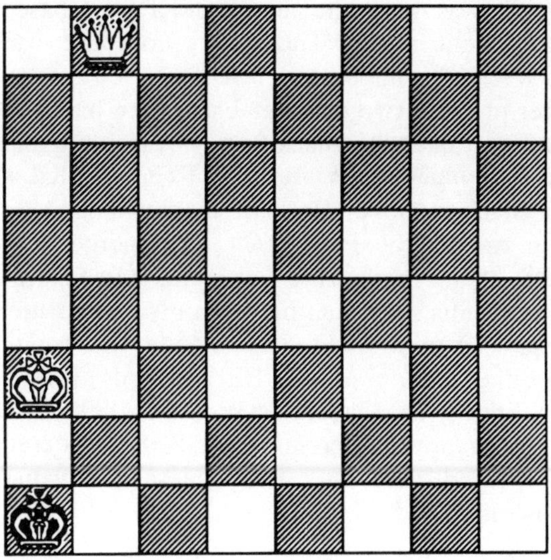

Figure 2.17 A stalemate. After White captures the BR shown in Figure 2.16 this stalemate occurs if White promotes the pawn to any piece that has a potential of winning (WR or WQ).

contain values for positions where the promoted white pawn is on rank 8. Unfortunately the same generation procedure requires that these databases report on Black-to-move values and Ken Thompson's databases contained values for White-to-move only.

A program was written which converted Thompson's (WFW/not WFW, White-to-move KQKR) database to a WFW/not WFW, WQ on rank 8, Black-to-move database (denoted KQ8KR), and generated every legal KQKR position with WQ on rank 8. From each of these positions every legal Black move was generated and looked up in the KQKR database. The worst value for White looked up in this database for the set

KQ8KR \ KR8KR	not won	won	illegal
not won	218 709	1	0
won	444 753	6709	0
illegal	0	0	378 404

Figure 2.18 KQ8KR and KR8KR BTM WFW/not WFW position tabulation. Note the presence of a position that is not WFW if the pawn is promoted to a queen but *is* WFW if the pawn is promoted to a rook.

of legal Black moves was put in the new (KQ8KR) database as the Black-to-move game theoretic value. The same procedure was applied to KRKR giving a KR8KR database.

The merger of these two new databases then had to be performed (i.e. the worst White-value with Black-to-move) resulting in the third and final derived database namely a White-value K(R or Q)KR with (R or Q) on rank 8 with Black-to-move. Each of the lookahead programs took about a week to run on the PDP 11/34. The merger took about two hours. The results of the merger are summarized in Figure 2.18.

The merger results show that there is only one position that is won for White if the pawn is promoted to a rook and is not won if promoted to a queen. This position (WK:c2 WR:c8 BK:a1 BR:d4) is on the move-line from a position known as Saavedra's position (1895) (WK:b6 WP:c6 BK:a1 BR:d5) and its appearance in Figure 2.18 lends credibility to the generated and merged database. The general problem of database generation is now discussed.

Chapter 3
Database Generation

3.1 The 'database' problem

Section 2.7 touched on the need for an alternative to 'dumb' search for generating chess databases. Two methods for cutting down the search space were suggested:

- throw away any illegal positions generated;
- use remembered value for any position previously encountered.

Throwing away illegal moves may reduce the average branching factor by a small amount. For KPKR the branching factor is between 8 and 10. The maximum depth of win is 38 ply, so a naive search would visit greater than 8^{38} nodes for every position to be evaluated (about 200 000 – 100 000 with Black-to-move and 100 000 with White-to-move) so small reductions in branching factor (of one or two) will make little impact on the search complexity. Far greater gains may be achieved by the sensible use of memory for partial result storage by exploiting the favourable space/time tradeoff, i.e. if the database generator is allowed to use memory, it will take less time to complete its task. More specifically, if the database generation algorithm has a storage slot allocated for every position in the KPK domain (about 200 000) it will not have to compute a value for any position more than once. Further gains can be made if the search space is limited to deal only with positions that lead to interesting positions (in our case these interesting positions were defined as those that are known to be won-for-White). This theme can be taken further: positions that lead to interesting positions are defined as interesting. Taken to its logical conclusion this theme (positions that eventually lead to positions that are won-for-White) defines a search strategy that is guaranteed to include all positions about which we would like to have some information. Ideally this information would be a number representing the depth of win. However, for the purposes of the experiments performed, just the fact that these positions are won-for-White is sufficient.

In order to implement the above search strategy one needs to be able to obtain (or generate) all initially interesting positions (for KPK this means the set of positions where White can *safely* promote to queen or rook (without creating stalemate) these are known as 'terminal' positions. One also needs a reverse legal move generator that can provide all legal predecessor positions to the one currently being investigated. Given these two resources the algorithm which is known as 'standard backup' database generation is now described.

3.2 Principles of standard backup database generation

The standard backup needs to be able to store two values for every position in the space, called depth and counter. These can be thought of as functions applied to a position P. Depth(P) returns the current depth of win associated with position P and is initially set to undefined. Counter(P) is only applied to BTM positions and returns the number of as yet untested Black moves from position P. Counter(P) where P is a BTM position is initially set to the number of legal Black moves from P. Having defined these two functions the standard backup algorithm is shown in Figure 3.1 (from Niblett, 1982). Note the choice of BTM positions as the initially evaluated positions is arbitrary.

Steps (1) to (3) are initialization and can be performed in one pass over the BTM and WTM positions. Steps (4) to (8) form the body of the

---

1. Set each BTM position P which is lost immediately as won-for-White depth 0 (depth(P) := 0). Set all other positions as undefined.
2. For each BTM position in the endgame set a counter containing the number of legal moves from that position.
3. Set i to 0.
4. For each BTM position P lost at depth i (depth(P) = i), generate its legal predecessors P_1, ..., P_i. If any P_j has depth(P_j) = undefined then set depth(P_j) := i + 1.
5. Set i := i + 1.
6. For each WTM position P that is won in depth i generate its legal predecessors P_1, ..., P_n. If any P_j has counter(P_j) = 1 and is not marked as won, then mark it won depth i + 1 (depth(P_j) := i + 1). Otherwise decrement the counter by 1 (counter(P_j) := counter(P_j) − 1).
7. Set i := i + 1.
8. Repeat steps (4) to (7) until no new positions are marked as won-for-white. All positions P from which White can force a win will have been set with depth(P) equal to some positive integer.

Figure 3.1 The standard backup algorithm. Note the choice of BTM positions as the initially evaluated positions is arbitrary.

algorithm and require a pass through these positions for every ply depth evaluated. Step (4) requires a linear search through WTM positions to find any that are lost in depth *i*. If these are BTM positions their predecessors must have been WTM so White must have had a move that caused Black to lose. White would surely make this move (given perfect play) so the game theoretic value from the WTM predecessor positions (there may be more than one) is won in depth i + 1.

Looking at WTM positions that are won depth i is more complicated. Since the predecessor of a WTM position is BTM, given perfect play, Black would not play a move that resulted in a won-for-White position unless there were no choice. So before the BTM predecessors can be marked as won depth i + 1, we must make sure there are no *other* moves Black may make that are not-won-for-White. If there were any then given perfect play, Black would surely make one of these. This is where the counter function comes in. Every BTM position is marked with the number of legal moves that Black can make. If for a given BTM predecessor to a won-for-White depth i position, this number is one then this is the only move Black can make and it must be won-for-White depth i + 1. If this number is two then there is another move Black can make so decrement counter(this BTM predecessor) by one (giving one). If in the future this position is backed-up to again, counter(this BTM predecessor) will be found to be one and this position will then be marked won-for-White depth i + 1. Note this value for i is not necessarily the same as it was when the position was first encountered as a BTM predecessor to a won-for-White position – it is probably greater. This is all right since, as it was a Black move and given perfect play, the game-theoretic value is the depth along the longest path that Black can delay a loss. Extending this explanation, if the value of counter (at some BTM position) is found to be N then there are $N - 1$ other positions that have this BTM position as a predecessor. Only if all $N - 1$ positions are backed-up to will a depth-of-win value be assigned to this BTM position. If not then depth(this BTM position) will remain undefined which means not-won-for-White.

Since for KPK the largest depth of win was found to be 38 ply, the algorithm needs about $38 \times 200\,000 = 7\,600\,000$ data accesses to complete the KPK database generation. Compared to the $8^{38} \times 200\,000$ accesses of a naive algorithm this represents a considerable saving and brings the task within the realms of feasibility. There are further savings to be made by making a clever cache of positions and incorporating some forward look-ahead in the backup search. One such algorithm was used for the generation of the KPa7KR database. The algorithm is shown in Figure 3.2. This algorithm is very much less disk-bound during execution than the standard algorithm of Figure 3.1. Note that the output of the algorithm for WTM positions does not give us access to the depth of win for these positions, only whether they are won or not.

Let MAX_MOVES be the maximum number of legal moves (enumerated in some standard order) possible from a BTM position (e.g. MAX_MOVES is 22 for KPKR). Moveno(P) is a counter which takes values in the range 0 to MAX_MOVES. It is used in the algorithm to keep track of which moves have been considered from BTM positions. We assume that initially decided positions are with BTM.

1. Set each BTM position P which is lost immediately as won-for-White depth 0 (depth(P) := 0). Set moveno(P) to be 0 for each BTM position P. Set all other positions as undefined.
2. Set i to 0.
3. For each BTM position P lost at depth i (depth(P) = i), generate its legal predecessors $P_1, \ldots, P_i$. If any P_j has depth(P_j) = undefined then set depth(P_j) := i + 1.
4. Set i := i + 1.
5. For each BTM position P not marked as lost – if the move represented by moveno(P) is illegal, impossible or leads to a WTM position increment moveno(P). If moveno(P) is incremented and moveno(P) < MAX_MOVES goto (5). If moveno(P) = MAX_MOVES all the possible moves from P are illegal or lead to lost positions so set depth(P) = i + 1.
6. Set i to i + 1.
7. If no new positions were marked as lost in step (3) or (5) then STOP else goto (3).

Figure 3.2 The backup algorithm modified to be less disk-bound. Note that the output of the algorithm for WTM positions does not give us access to the depth of win for these positions, only whether they are won or not.

3.3 Difficulties and pitfalls

The main difficulties are concerned with, firstly, finding all terminal positions (this process for KPa7KR has been described and was by no means easy) and, secondly, ensuring that the reverse legal move generator works in strange cases, e.g. it is easy to forget that some positions are impossible to get to, bad data may be generated for positions backing-up to them. Since mistakes cost many CPU hours, trial and error is not a feasible approach. So modular design and testing is essential. Fortunately the algorithm is straightforward.

3.4 The checking problem

Having generated a database the problem of how to test it remains to be solved. The testing method with mathematical tables might be to take some random sample (or all entries if the table is 'small'), compute the tabulated function and check it against the corresponding database entry. However, with these 'complex' chess endgames there is in general *no* feasible computation of the tabulated function.

A very cheap check is to examine statistics like those obtained for the K(Q8 or R8)KR terminal position database. The rediscovery of Saavedra's position was a useful source of confidence (but hardly a foolproof test of database integrity).

A partial solution to this problem (making do) is to get someone else independently to attempt the database generation and then compare the databases 'byte for byte'. This is costly in resources and still does not guarantee that both generators have not made the same mistakes. Fortunately the generation algorithm is reasonably simple. But conceptual mistakes can and do creep in that would not be obvious to human designers of database generators.

The approach we took was as follows. The database was to be used as a checking device for other solutions (inductively derived from a chess master as oracle) for the same problem (KPKR White-to-move with WP:a7). It would not be begging the question too much to use each to cross-check the other. The idea is that each may show up whole classes of errors in the other and the chance that each would contain exactly the same members of a given class of error as misclassified should be remote (since each uses a very different evaluation technique). The pitfall of this approach occurs if a detected error is treated in isolation from its class (as an exception) without finding its 'class cause'.

Endgame	Subset	Legal positions	Number of +ve outcome	Max depth to outcome (moves)	Database size (bytes)
KPK	WP:[a-d][2-7]	BTM 83 622	48 795 WFW	19	98 304
KPK	pawn-can-run	BTM 83 622	36 958	5	98 304
KPK	WP:a[2-7]	BTM 20 919	12 312 WFW	10	24 576
KPK	main pattern	BTM 31 185	12 796	19	49 152
KPK	WP:[a-d][5-6]	BTM 21 012	9 765	14	32 768
KPK	WP:[a-d]7	BTM 10 506	237	2	16 384
KQKR	WQ:?8	BTM 670 172	451 462 WFW	31	1 892 352
KRKR	WR:?8	BTM 670 172	6 710 WFW	3	1 892 352
KPKR	WP:a7	209 718	129 825 WFW	†	262 144
KPKR	WP:b7	206 424	124 782 WFW	†	262 144

† Since the KPa7KR database was generated using the modified backup algorithm, this information is not available.

Figure 3.3 Databases generated during the course of this research. Note: If won versus not-won information is all that is required, database sizes given in bytes can be regarded as their size in bits.

Database	Number of positions at maximum depth	Example position at maximum depth			
KPK (pawn-can-run)	4628 (5)	WK:a1	WP:a2	BK:d1	
KPK (WP:a[2-7])	21 (10)	WK:b2	WP:a2	BK:d2	
KPK (main pattern)	1 (19)	WK:h3	WP:b2	BK:h5	
KPK (WP:[a-d][5-6])	41 (14)	WK:f4	WP:b2	BK:f8	
KPK (WP:[a-d]7)	237 (2)	WK:a6	WP:b7	BK:c6	
KQKR (BTM WQ:?8)	11 (31)	WK:a8	WQ:d8	BK:c3	BR:b4
KRKR (BTM WR:?8)	3 (3)	WK:a1	WR:a8	BK:a3	BR:c2

Figure 3.4 Some database statistics. The numbers in brackets are the maximum depth of wins (in moves) as given in the previous figure.

An error in the database was found in this way and it was indeed one that another database builder might well have overlooked. It was the stalemate position given in the previous chapter (WK:a3 WP:a7 BK:a1 BR:b8). This position was mistakenly included in the set of terminal positions as won-for-White. The consequences were not too disastrous for the rest of the database.

It may be wondered how such a mistake could be made? The possibility of stalemate was considered and rejected since it was assumed that White could always avoid the draw by minimally underpromoting the pawn (i.e. to rook). In this case underpromotion does no good. If it is minimal, then stalemate occurs. If underpromotion is not minimal (i.e. to knight or bishop) the win fails from insufficient force.

3.5 Databases generated for the present work

Figure 3.3 shows a table of databases generated during the course of this research. Some further analysis yields the table shown in Figure 3.4. From these tables it can be seen that the deepest KPK win-for-White with BTM is a position within the main pattern subproblem namely WK:h3 WP:b2 BK:h5 and is solved in 19 moves.

Chapter 4

Techniques in the Use of Computer Induction

4.1 Structured induction

Established programming techniques dictate that when faced with a complex programming task, the problem to be solved should be split into smaller more manageable subproblems. Each subproblem is usually programmed as a procedure, and procedures can typically be nested to any level. The precise choice and hierarchical order of subproblems is the product of top-down design (as in **structured programming**). We call the induction method developed from this idea by Shapiro and Niblett (1982) **structured induction**.

With computer induction the same human-generated top-down problem decomposition can be combined with bottom-up implementation of the bodies of the individual procedures, using example-value pairs obtained from an oracle, e.g. from an expert in the domain of the given procedure. The domain expert decides on the attributes that he knows to have most bearing on the problem to be solved. He takes each one of these in turn and, in consultation with a programmer, they decide if these attributes are immediately codable. If any are not then the decomposition process is repeated for each attribute that is not immediately codable until none is left. This produces a hierarchical tree of subproblems whose leaf nodes are directly codable attributes.

The next stage involves using inductive inference to solve each of the subproblems from the bottom of this hierarchy to the top. Interactive ID3 is applied to each subproblem in each hierarchical level in turn and a decision tree (in the form of a compilable function) for each is produced and tuned until the domain expert is satisfied that each deals with all the example situations that he intended they should when the problem decomposition was being performed.

This process of tuning involves the expert using the current rule to classify examples other than those so far used in the rule-training process. Failures to classify correctly a new example fall into two categories:

- examples that result in clashing decision-vectors (i.e. same attribute values but different class values), either caused by an incorrectly classified example or an incorrectly defined or missing attribute; and

- examples that contradict the current rule.

A clash can be dealt with either by removing the incorrectly classified example (if any) or by redefining the faulty attribute. An example that contradicts the current rule indicates that the rule needs to be re-induced with this example included in the training set. The expert also has some control over the order in which attributes appear in the rule. In the case of a tie in the measure that is used to sequence attributes within a rule, their order of appearance in the attribute description file is used.

Each newly solved subproblem is then given a meaningful name which is used in the next level up as a simple codable attribute. Each induced solution is now a directly executable piece of code that, when run, delivers a value that has the expert's seal of approval. This process is continued until there are no more subproblem hierarchy levels to ascend (the top of the decomposition tree has been reached).

At this stage a top-level problem exists that, when run, calls the lower level subproblems and attributes in an order determined by the inductive procedures applied at each level of the bottom-up implementation.

For example, consider the following problem 'p' that an expert has decided is best split by attributes a_1, a_2 and a_3. Since it is decided that both a_2 and a_3 are too complicated to be coded as attributes, they are treated as subproblems and the expert splits a_2 using attributes a_{21}, a_{22}, a_{23} and a_{24}, and a_3 is split using attributes a_{31} and a_{32}. The top-down problem decomposition is shown in Figure 4.1 (circled items are subproblems and boxed items are directly codable attributes).

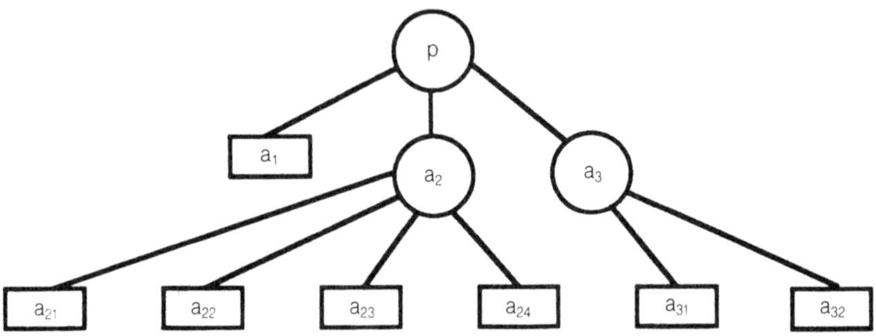

Figure 4.1 Top-down decomposition of hypothetical problem 'p'. It should be noted that although attributes are shown as distinct entities there is no reason why they should not be functionally equivalent; for example in the above tree the nodes a_{21} and a_{32} might correspond to identically the same test. This is demonstrated, for example, in the KPa7KR experiment (described later) where the attribute r2ar8 appears several times in the structured solution.

This completes the expert's hierarchical decomposition. (Note that the only ordering information contained in this decomposition tree is the depth at which a subproblem will be executed. There is no horizontal ordering implied.)

A programmer now codes the four procedures corresponding to attributes $a_{2[1-4]}$ and the expert uses Interactive ID3 to produce a rule that he likes (by providing relevant examples and suggesting attribute coding changes to the programmer). Suppose the expert-approved rule is as shown in Figure 4.2 (the decision classes are called a_2D1 and a_2D2), and when the process is repeated for a_3, the rule produced is as shown in Figure 4.3.

These rules are then substituted for a_2 and a_3 respectively. Interactive ID3 is once again applied and the resulting rule (shown in Figure 4.4) is the solution to the original problem 'p'.

```
if a24
    then a2D1
else if a21
    then a2D2
else
    a2D1
```

Figure 4.2 Hypothetical expert-approved rule for a_2.

```
if a32
    then a3D1
else if a31
    then a3D2
else
    a3D1
```

Figure 4.3 Hypothetical expert approved rule for a_3.

```
if a2 = a2D1
    then pD1
else if a3 = a3D1
    then pD2
else if a1 = a1D1
    then pD1
else
    pD2
```

Figure 4.4 The top-level solution to the original problem 'p'.

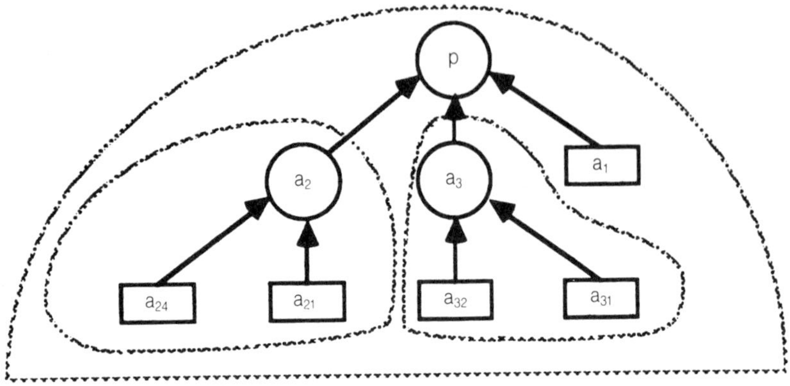

Figure 4.5 Decomposition diagram for hypothetical problem 'p'. A left-to-right depth-first execution ordering is implied.

We can now reproduce the problem decomposition diagram with irrelevant attributes removed and an implied left-to-right depth-first execution ordering as shown in Figure 4.5. Notice that if elements of the same decision tree are enclosed (as in this figure) in a separate envelope (dotted lines), then the whole structure maps in an obvious way on to a program in a hypothetical programming language, as shown in Figure 4.6. This correspondence is taken up in Chapter 8 where a description may be found of the CDL-1 rule language which took its origin from the present work.

4.2 Self-commenting

Based on a proposal by D. Michie, self-commenting is a programming technique by which a humanly understandable commentary is generated whenever the induced rule executes on a test example. This feature has two main uses: rule debugging and answering the 'why did you decide that?' question at rule execution time.

When debugging a rule (or subproblem) such a commentary is helpful since it shows the expert at a glance which attribute is giving the wrong result. Self-commenting was used to debug an inductively synthesized KPa7KR rule (see Figure 7.40). After synthesis from 325 expert-supplied tutorial examples, a complete database became available of the 209 718 legal KPa7KR positions. Of these, 15 were found to be incorrectly classified by the rule. It took only two hours to correct these errors. On earlier occasions it had taken approximately 20 times longer to correct errors of comparable subtlety.

The execution-time use has an impact on the problem of human understandability of automatically generated rules. It is not enough to

p	—	program
a_2 then a_3 then a_1	—	body of p
a_2	—	procedure
a_3	—	procedure
a_1	—	primitive procedure
a_{24} then a_{21}	—	body of a_2
a_{32} then a_{31}	—	body of a_3
a_{24}	—	primitive procedure
a_{21}	—	primitive procedure
a_{32}	—	primitive procedure
a_{31}	—	primitive procedure

Figure 4.6 'p' mapped on to a hypothetical programming language.

inform someone that a particular rule has been vetted by an expert and is to be trusted. It is also not enough to present the rule as the definitive text on a problem and expect an inexperienced user to gain an expert's insight by inspection of this rule. He requires in addition the freedom to inspect the line of inference whereby the rule-base has arrived at its conclusion.

For self-commenting to work, the expert must insert a question text at the entry point of each problem, subproblem and primitive attribute, and also plant at each exit point a corresponding answer text (e.g. YES, NO). At rule-execution time, the question text corresponding to each activated subproblem and attribute is output before the subproblem or attribute is executed. The question text is kept in the attribute description file where it also acts as a natural language description for the symbolic name given to attributes and subproblems listed in such files.

For example, consider the attribute katri from the KPa7KR experiment found in subproblem dblat. katri is described in the dblat attribute description file the relevant line of which is shown in Figure 4.7. When Interactive ID3 forms a rule using this attribute it uses this information as shown in Figure 4.8.

This is only half of the commentary text available to the self-commenting system. The other half is the answers to the questions posed at subproblem and attribute entry. These answers are stored at the exit points of the coded attributes and subproblems. If self-commenting is enabled, the text corresponding to the relevant return point is output,

```
katri 3 B W N    Does any king control intersect point. If so, which
```

Figure 4.7 A fragment of the dblat attribute description file.

```
enter("katri", "Does any king control intersect point. If so, which", LEVEL);
switch(katri()) {
  case B:
    etc.
}
```

Figure 4.8 A fragment of the dblat decision rule. The function enter is a compile-time option that, when enabled, causes its first two arguments to be printed and a question mark to be inserted. LEVEL is a compile-time constant that causes the question to be printed at an indent level corresponding to depth of the subproblem or attribute in the decomposition tree.

```
katri() {
  if(bitset(wf, wr, IS_INTERSECT))
    return(comment(E, "%", "", "", "NO the WK is in check", LEVEL));
  or(BKING, BATT, 20);
  or(WKING, WATT, 22);
  and(IS_INTERSECT, 20, 21);
  and(IS_INTERSECT, 22, 23);
  if(!zero(21)) {
    if(zero(23))
      return(comment(B, "%s", "YES the BK does", "", "", LEVEL));
    return(comment(E, "%s", "", "", "NO both do", LEVEL));
  }
  if(!zero(23))
    return(comment(W, "%s", "", "YES the WK does", "", LEVEL));
  return(comment(E, "%s", "", "", "NO none do", LEVEL));
}
```

Figure 4.9 C code for attribute katri. The function comment is a compile-time option that is replaced by its first argument if comments are disabled. Otherwise it causes one of three strings to be output depending on the run-time value of its first argument. If these string slots are empty, the default action is to print out a simple YES/NO answer.

forming a question–answer dialogue. For example, consider the C code for katri (shown in Figure 4.9) – the attribute used in the previous example.

The same commenting convention must be maintained when Interactive ID3 generates compilable code for a subproblem. This subproblem must call comment when it executes a return and the comment that is output must be displayed at a lower indent level since it answers the question that preceded the call to this subproblem. Part of Interactive ID3's output was shown in Figure 4.8, the rest of Interactive ID3's treatment of the call to the katri attribute is shown in Figure 4.10.

```
enter("katri", "Does any king control intersect point. If so, which", LEVEL);
switch(katri(LEVEL)) {
  case B:
    return(comment(TRUE, FALSE, "", "", "", LEVEL–1));
    break;
  case W:
    return(comment(FALSE, FALSE, "", "", "", LEVEL–1));
    break;
  default:
    etc.
}
```

Figure 4.10 Use of katri in the automatically generated C-coded decision rule.

The self-commenting output from the induced KPa7KR rule for position WK:g8 WP:a7 BK:c7 BR:d4 (which is critically dependent on the value of katri) is shown in Figure 4.11. (The output that results from code given earlier as examples is shown in italics.)

4.3 Post-processing self-commentary texts

Let us now consider how this text might be reorganized (e.g. by a post-processor) so as to avoid the deep nesting structure and associated postponement of answers to questions which are high up in that structure. These features have arisen because of the convention that explanatory text should appear in exactly the same order as that of their run-time invocation. Perhaps, then, we should experiment with ways of relaxing this convention, so as to generate explanatory text with a more event-driven flavour.

A transformation which may be useful for this purpose is analogous to that used to convert ordinary bracketed (infix) algebraic/arithmetic functional expressions into 'reverse Polish' (postfix) expressions. By this transformation an expression of the form:

$$(a + b) \times c$$

which needs brackets because of the implied precedence of × over +, becomes:

$$ab + c \times$$

which is executed in a strictly left-to-right order on a one-address machine (i.e. a machine with no memory except a stack) as shown in Figure 4.12.

The infix expression, corresponding to the self-commented text shown in Figure 4.11, is shown in Figure 4.13. The same expression is

Is this position won-for-White? (pa7)
  Can the BR be captured safely? (rimmx)
  NO
  Does one or more B piece control the queening square? (bxqsq)
  NO
  Is the WK in stalemate? (stlmt)
  NO
  Is there a good delayed skewer threat? (ds)
    Is there a special opposition pattern present? (spcop)
    NO
    Is the WK one away from the relevant edge? (wtoeg)
    NO
  NO
  Is there a simple delay to White's queening the pawn? (dq)
    Is there a good delay because there is a mate threat? (thrmt)
      Does the BR attack a mating square safely? (rxmsq)
      NO because there is no mating square
    NO
    Is there a good delay because the WK is on square a8? (wka8d)
      Is the WK on square a8? (wkna8)
      NO
    NO
    Is there a good delay because the WK is in check? (wkchk)
      Is the WK in check? (wknck)
      NO
    NO
    Is there a good delay because of a double attack threat? (dblat)
      Is the WK on an edge and not on a8? (cntxt)
      YES
      Is the BK in the way? (bkblk)
      NO
      Is the BK attacked in some way by the promoted WP? (bkxbq)
      NO
      Does any king control intersect point. If so, which? (katri)
      YES the BK does
    YES
  YES
NO

Figure 4.11 Self-commenting output for position WK:g8 WP:a7 BK:c7 BR:d4. The output that results from code given earlier as examples is shown in italics.

```
STACK a
STACK b
ADD          (the top 2 items on the stack, replacing them with the answer)
STACK c
MULTIPLY     (the top 2 items on the stack, replacing them with the answer)
```

Figure 4.12 Execution of the postfix expression $ab + c \times$.

```
PA7(rimmx bxqsq stlmt DS(spcop wtoeg) DQ(thrmt(rxmsq) WKA8D(wkna8)
WKCHK(wknck) DBLAT(cntxt bkblk bkxbq katri)))
```

Figure 4.13 Infix form for self-commented text shown in Figure 4.11. To avoid bulk only the attribute names not the explanation text are used. The non-primitives are capitalized for ease of identification.

```
katri bkxbq bkblk cntxt DBLAT wknck WKCHK wkna8 WKA8D rxmsq THRMT
DQ wtoeg spcop DS stlmt bxqsq rimmx PA7
```

Figure 4.14 Postfix form for self-commented text shown in Figure 4.13. The non-primitives (operators in the postfix expression) are capitalized for ease of identification.

shown in postfix form in Figure 4.14. The subproblems themselves are treated as operators. They are applied to the contents of the stack on which they leave their result.

This postfix expression could be used to generate an 'after the event' explanation like the one shown in Figure 4.15.

A further refinement of the self-commenting idea suggested by Ivan Bratko would optionally condense the commentaries by omitting print-out of strings associated with tests which are redundant to predicting the outcome *given the current rule*. This regime was modified to make an exception always of the last subproblem to be invoked as shown in Figure 4.16.

This last form is not useful when the commentary is being used to debug the rule (due to the loss of information about other tests that were made). However, providing the rule is an accepted orderly solution to the problem this terse form of reporting can be of use as a 'to-the-point' explanation. If the reader has in his head a variant rule with reference to which not all the omitted tests are redundant, then in principle he might perceive the explanation as in some way lacking. Equally there could be

seeing that the BK controls the intersect point
    when the BK is not attacked in some way by the promoted WP
    and the BK is not in the way
    and the WK is on an edge and not on a8
it follows that there is a good delay because of a double attack threat

seeing that the WK is not in check
it follows that there is not a good delay because the WK is in check

seeing that the WK is not on square a8
it follows that there is not a good delay because the WK is on square a8

seeing that the BR does not attack a mating square safely
it follows that there is not a good delay because there is a mate threat

seeing that there is a good delay because of a double attack threat
    when there is not a good delay because the WK is in check
    and there is not a good delay because the WK is on square a8
    and there is not a good delay because there is a mate threat
it follows that there is a simple delay to queening the pawn

seeing that the WK is not one away from the relevant edge
    when there is not a special opposition pattern present
it follows that there is not a good delayed skewer threat

seeing that there is a simple delay to White's queening the pawn
    when there is not a good delayed skewer threat
    and the WK is not in stalemate
    and one or more B piece does not control the queening square
    and the BR cannot be captured safely
it follows that this position is not won for White

Figure 4.15 A postfix 'after-the-event' explanation text.

seeing that the BK controls the intersect point
    when the BK is not attacked in some way by the promoted WP
    and the BK is not in the way
    and the WK is on an edge and not on a8
it follows that there is a good delay because of a double attack threat
from this it follows that there is a simple delay to White's queening the pawn
from this it follows that this position is not won for White

Figure 4.16 'To-the-point' postfix self-commenting.

tests in the text which according to his own rule should have been omitted. The extent to which consumer dissatisfaction from this cause will be encountered is not yet known. The remedy is in any case immediate, since the user is free to switch to one of the unabridged options.

Comment was invited from Dr D. Kopec, a US National (FIDE) Master and former Scottish Chess Champion, on the three variant forms for the specimen worked example:

1. infix;
2. postfix; and
3. abbreviated postfix.

They are given in Figures 4.11, 4.15 and 4.16. His clearly expressed preference placed them in the order (3), (2), (1). Dr Kopec felt in fact that the abbreviated postfix form promised to be fully adequate to the needs of the run-time expert user.

The post-processor described here has been implemented as a program in the language C (Shapiro and Michie, 1986). Problems of natural language processing were avoided by the use of a human-generated auxiliary text file containing the correct English phrases for negations whose use might be deemed necessary at run-time.

Chapter 5

Plan of the Experiments

Two main experiments were performed:

- KPK (BTM); and
- KPKR (WP:a7 WTM).

5.1 The first experiment

The aim of the first experiment (KPK) was partly to determine whether or not inductive learning techniques were applicable to reasonably complex problems. In this respect the work was largely confirmatory of that done by Quinlan (1979). New ground was, however, broken by the introduction of the 'brain-compatibility' criterion and of the structured induction technique designed to meet it. It was felt that quantitative information on the cost of manufacturing a solution by induction was needed. Part of the KPK investigation concerned transparency of solutions. The experiment was split into two inductive learning experiments (structured and unstructured) and a database lookup program, which performed the same function as the induced rules, was added to give a comparison. Both structured and unstructured synthesis made full use of the available databases. No expert-directed learning took place (except in the choice of attributes and subproblems). The main aim of this experiment was to compare the costs associated with the synthesis and the execution of rules produced by the two styles of computer induction – unstructured (as in Quinlan) and structured.

The task of the expert (Dr T. Niblett) for this experiment was to partition the problem as he deemed necessary and then to aid in the choice of attributes. He also had to examine clashing examples as they

<long-legs, spotted, long-neck, herbivore, GIRAFFE>
<long-legs, spotted, long-neck, herbivore, NOT–GIRAFFE>.

Figure 5.1 A clash.

arose and suggest the cause. Recall that a clash exists if a set of two or more decision-vectors agree in all values of the attributes but not in the decision-class value. Figure 5.1 shows a clash.

5.2 The second experiment

The aim of the second experiment (KPa7KR) was to solve a problem using inductive inference that was considered too complex to be hand coded, and furthermore to solve it without the use of a database. WTM was chosen because the previously solved KPK BTM problem is a derived endgame (WK capturing BR results in a BTM KPK game). It was decided to restrict the initial position of the WP to the most difficult single square on the board (a7) as an initial simplification (though still comprising over 200 000 legal positions) and to restrict the outcome values to be won-/not-won-for-White (as opposed to won/lost/drawn). This last simplification was to facilitate the generation of a checking database without which no quantitative results would be definitive. By subsequently adding a 'lost-for-White' solution (Shapiro, 1983, Appendix C) a complete won–drawn–lost classifier was achieved.

Several experts were used for this experiment. Each provided a very useful cross-check on the other. Where possible they were kept from consulting each other so that their approaches were independent. In the USA Rob Gordon and Marcel Schoppers in a University of Illinois graduate class project (supervised by the author) provided the top-down problem decomposition and the attributes, debugging these until they could detect no mistakes. At this point the resulting decision trees were saved for future evaluation against a database (which was not yet available). These decision trees will be referred to as 'stage one' in the results section (Shapiro, 1983, Appendix B contains the project report generated from this stage of the research). All three 'experts' were far from expert in the unrestricted game of chess, being probably 'B' players. However, KPa7KR is a small enough subgame for expertise to be acquirable, as experience showed.

The Gordon/Schoppers/Shapiro solution was brought back to the UK where Dr Kopec was asked to supply examples that he considered representative of the KPa7KR problem with a view to 'breaking' the current decision rule. Dr Kopec supplied examples in groups of about 90 thereby bringing to light a total of 23 'bugs'. After the decision trees were debugged against each group of examples supplied by Dr Kopec they were saved for future evaluation against a database (not available at this stage). Dr Kopec supplied altogether 263 examples (of which 39 were duplicates) and the decision trees will be referred to as stages two to four in the results section.

The 'lost-for-White' problem has subsequently been solved as part of a class project at the University of Illinois by R. Reinke (supervised by the author) but since the 'value-for-black' database has not been completed at this time, the exact performance of this module although believed high is unknown. Using the tools described previously Reinke arrived at his solution in under two weeks of non-dedicated time. The won-for-White solution, together with the lost-for-White solution, provides a complete solution for the three valued KPKR (WP:a7, WTM) problem, since if not-won-for-White and not-lost-for-White then a position must be drawn. More recently he has solved WFW/not WFW WP:b7 (again without the use of a database). This solution was found to be 94.8% correct against MIRU's KPKR database (Shapiro, 1983, Appendix C contains his project report).

Chapter 6

KPK Experiment

6.1 Introduction to the topic

The KPK endgame is one of the more elementary chess endgames, yet contains a surprising degree of complexity. It is very hard to program using a conventional tree search plus evaluation function since the maximum depth of win is 38 ply, leaving much domain-specific knowledge to be incorporated in the evaluation function. This allots to the programmer the task of dealing with the many exceptional positions that arise. In this environment it can take months to produce a correct program. Zuidema (1974) gives a good description of the programming problems that can arise from the 'exceptions nuisance' with an even simpler ending (KRK) which he was (eventually) able to solve on a no-search basis.

Several attempts have been made to program KPK using a more modular and knowledge-based approach. We shall describe the play of KPK as given in the textbook *Pawn Endings* (Averbakh and Maizelis, 1974) where a particularly lucid exposition is given. Following this we describe a top-level strategy developed by Dr T. Niblett (1982). Although developed for WTM KPK positions this strategy formed the basis of the structured induction experiments performed on BTM KPK positions.

6.2 The play of KPK

The play of KPK is determined by two considerations:

- the square of the pawn; and
- the pawn's critical squares.

The square of the pawn is shown in Figure 6.1. When the pawn's rank is less than 5 the critical squares are as shown in Figure 6.2, otherwise as in Figure 6.3. If the white king can occupy one of the critical squares White wins whoever is to move.

Averbakh treats the rookpawn as a special case, with only one critical square, the location of which is independent of the pawn, as shown in Figure 6.4.

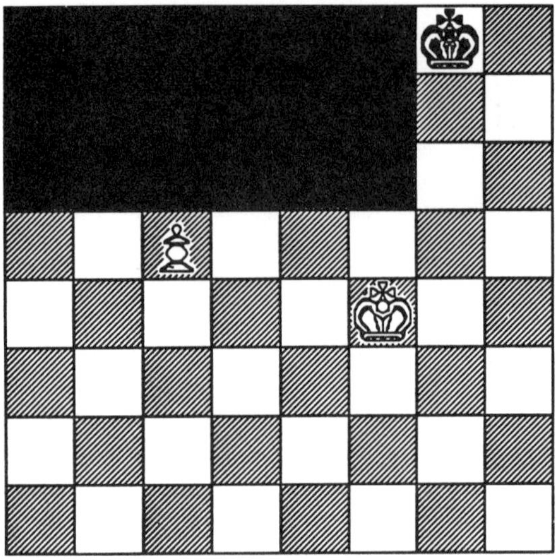

Figure 6.1 The square of the pawn. With White-to-move (WTM) the pawn advances, the square contracts and the black king cannot move into the new square, allowing the white pawn to queen safely. With BTM the black king can enter the square and so prevent the pawn queening.

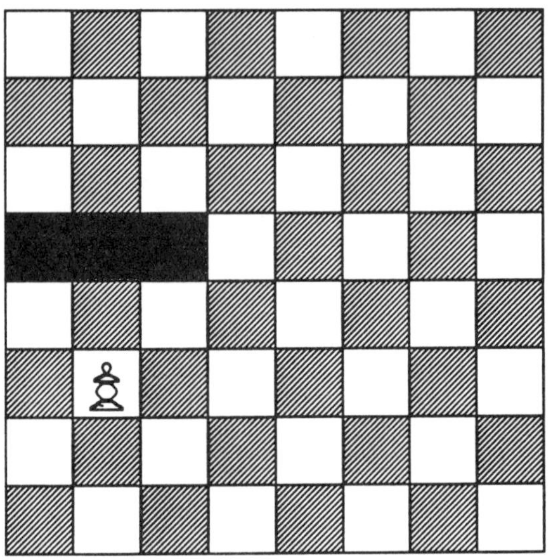

Figure 6.2 The critical squares of the pawn with the pawn's rank < 5.

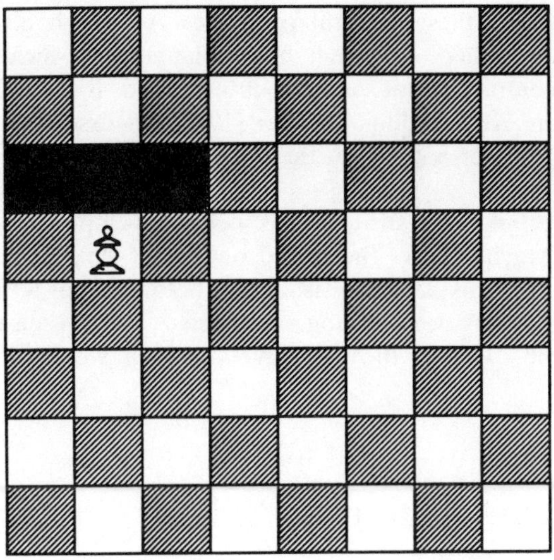

Figure 6.3 The critical squares of the pawn with the pawn's rank >= 5.

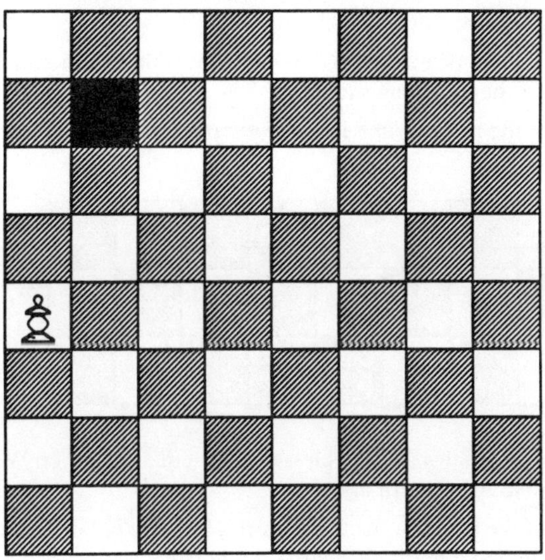

Figure 6.4 The rookpawn's critical square.

To accompany these general principles Averbakh gives about a dozen examples of play. Although his explanation is lucid, and to a human player complete, not enough information is given to specify correct play in the KPK ending. Bramer (1977) discusses this point. The task of the programmer is to fill in the details, producing a program that plays correctly.

An advice language strategy has been developed at the MIRU (Niblett, 1982) which follows the broad outline of Averbakh's text. An English version of this strategy is given below. The KPK game is effectively split into a variety of subgames each of which is easier than the whole KPK game. This is the strategy on which we have based our experiments.

6.3 A top-level strategy for KPK

To determine whether White wins from any WTM position, consider the rules shown in Figure 6.5 in order.

- If the pawn can run White wins.
- Otherwise if the pawn is a rookpawn White wins if a position is achievable where the pawn can run.
- Otherwise if the pawn's rank is 7 White wins if the white king can safely move next to the queening square.
- Otherwise if the pawn's rank is 6 and the pattern shown below holds White wins.

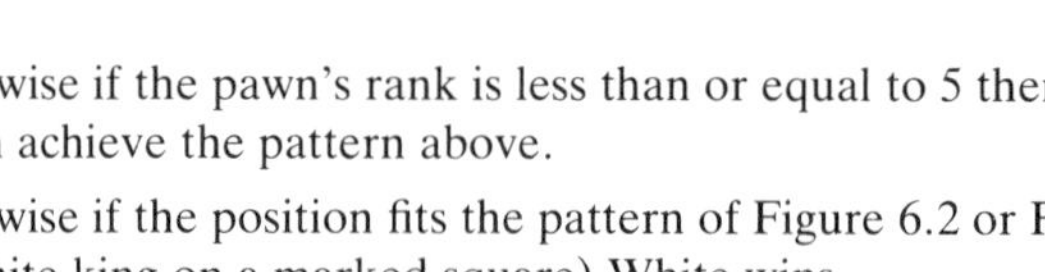

- Otherwise if the pawn's rank is less than or equal to 5 then White wins if he can achieve the pattern above.
- Otherwise if the position fits the pattern of Figure 6.2 or Figure 6.3 (with the white king on a marked square) White wins.
- Otherwise White wins if the pattern of Figure 6.2 or Figure 6.3 (with the white king on a marked square) is achievable.

Figure 6.5 Rules for White to win from any WTM KPK position.

6.4 Previous computer work

The history of earlier work on this endgame has been reviewed by Kopec (1982). The main milestones which he discusses are the following:

1977 M.R.B. Clarke's complete lookup database for KPK. For each position the won/drawn status was given and the depth of win or draw (e.g. the depth at which Black captures the WP). A complete statistical tabulation was given.

1975 L. Harris's Algol 60 search-oriented program classified positions with approximately 98% accuracy (as later shown by Bitner and Hansche, 1976).

1977 D. Beal's exceptionally fast and compact won/drawn classifier took the form of a decision table comprising 48 rules. These proved to be completely opaque to human inspection, even though correct and highly effective. The algorithm did not include move generation or depth information.

1977 M. Bramer wrote a pattern-based program comprising some 20 rules which made the best White move from any KPK WTM position. In the realm of KPK this miniature 'expert system' is the example *par excellence* of the classical knowledge engineering approach of extracting rules from the expert for codification and testing. In this case extraction proceeded by introspection, since domain expert and programmer were the same person.

6.5 Structured induction of decision rules

The size of the KPK problem space must be discussed, partly because previous published statements on this subject have not been entirely unambiguous or free from error. The figure (97 992) for the number of legal BTM positions that is usually quoted (Clarke, 1977) includes as legal 390 positions that have no legal White-to-move predecessor. There are 388 such positions where the black king is in check when the pawn is on the second rank, e.g. WK:c1 WP:a2 BK:b3. The point is that the pawn could not have moved to place the black king in check. The other two positions are when the only possible white predecessor moves were king moves from illegal positions, e.g. WK:a1 WP:a2 BK:c1 (BK:c2 generates the other example). That brings the size of the space down to 97 602. This figure includes 13 980 pawn on rank 8 positions which, according to our convention here, are no longer within the KPK subdomain. Thus the figure for the number of legal KPK positions with BTM that is used in this paper is 83 622.

The aim was to produce fairly simple decision trees, reflecting the domain expert's intuitive feel for the structure of the various subproblems. We will discuss the individual cases, giving our conclusions at the end. All attributes marked with * are evaluated using the CLIP/C emulator. All attributes marked with ○ are subproblems.

6.6 KPK problem decomposition tree

Referring to the figure opposite, subproblems are circled, primitive attributes are boxed.

6.7 Subproblem 1: pawn-can-run

The pawn can run in a position if the pawn can safely advance to the queening square without moving the white king. Of the 83 622 legal BTM positions, 36 958 are positions where the pawn can run. This subproblem can be solved by a 9 ply search involving up to 30 000 nodes using a naive depth first algorithm.

The final attribute set was:

1. wkahd *: The white king is ahead of the pawn.
2. stlmt *: Either the black king is in stalemate, or advancing the pawn forces stalemate.
3. ahead *: The black king can get ahead of the pawn on the pawn's file, before the eighth rank. The black king is not allowed to move on to squares the white king attacks.
4. plus1 *: The distance of the pawn to the queening square is greater than the black king's effective distance plus one.
5. plus2 *: The distance of the pawn to the queening square is greater than the black king's effective distance plus two.
6. imcap *: The black king can immediately capture the pawn.
7. patt1: This corresponds to a special edge case illustrated below. The black king is constrained to retreat, allowing the pawn to run.

8. crit *: The white king has control over the seventh rank square covering the queening square on the black king's side of the pawn.

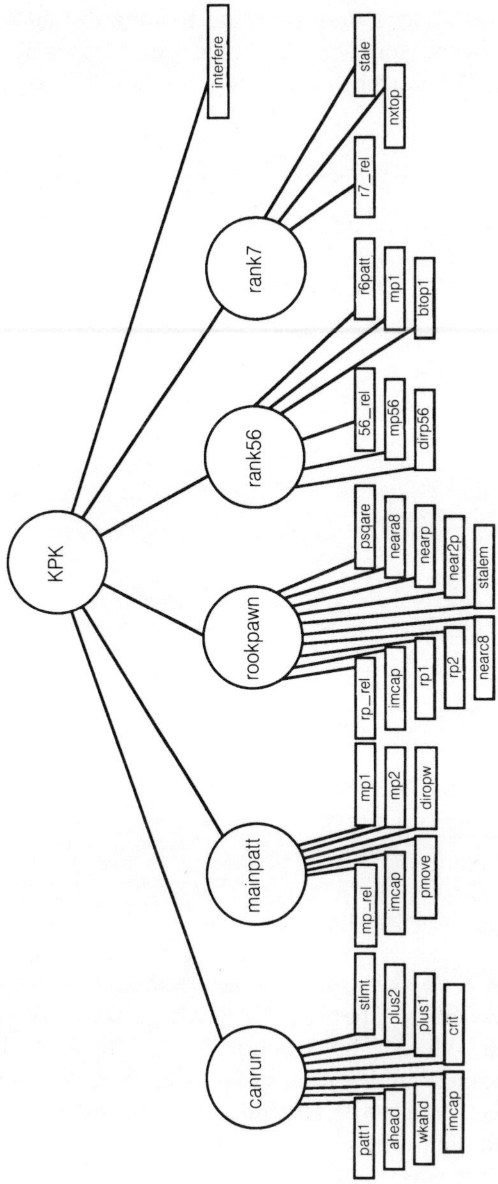

KPK problem decomposition tree
2-level structure
5 subproblems
34 attributes (31 unique)
83 622 legal positions (BTM)
48 795 WFW 34 827 DRAWN

The black king's effective distance from Square1 to Square2 is defined as the minimum pathlength of the black king from Square1 to Square2 with all the squares attacked by the white king disallowed. If no such path exists the effective distance is set equal to a large number. Effective distance is always greater than or equal to king distance. The attributes stlmt and patt1 were added to take account of special cases arising from edge effects. The machine-generated decision rule is shown in Figure 6.6.

No. of examples in final working-set = 16.
No. of nodes in final tree = 17.
Time taken to generate rule = 0.60 CPU second.

```
patt1
  f: ahead
    f: wkahd
      f: imcap
        f: stlmt
          f: plus2
            t: plus1
              f: crit
                f: FALSE
                t: TRUE
              t: FALSE
            f: TRUE
          t: FALSE
        t: FALSE
      t: FALSE
    t: FALSE
  t: TRUE
```

Figure 6.6 pawn-can-run decision tree.

6.8 Subproblem 2: rookpawn

Positions where the pawn is on the rook's file are treated as a particular subproblem, following Averbakh. There are 20 919 legal BTM rookpawn positions, 12 312 won for White. This was the most difficult problem, probably because Averbakh's guidelines were inadequate. We needed eight iterations to produce a clash-free attribute set. The initial attribute set had four elements, the final one ten.

The final attribute set was:

1. rookpawn_relevant: Is pawn on rook's file and not able to run.
2. nearc8 *: The black king can reach c8 before the white king.
3. neara8 *: The black king can reach a8 before the white king.

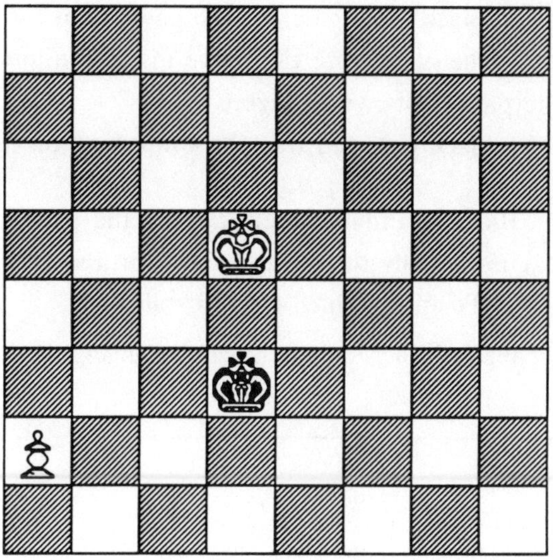

Figure 6.7 rookpawn pattern 1 (rp1). BK–›c3 (to get near enough to the WP to capture it). If WP–›a4 then BK–›b4 will win the WP. If instead of WP–›a4, White plays WK–›c5 then BK–›b4 or BK–›b3 are illegal (BK moves into check). The nearest the BK can get to the WP is b2 but then WP–›a4 allows the WP to beat the BK to the 'queening square'.

Figure 6.8 Can the BK get next to the WP? (near2p). BK–›d3 (to get near enough to the WP to capture it). If WP–›a4 then BK–›c4 will ensure that the WP doesn't escape. If instead of WP–›a4, White plays WK–›d5 then BK–›c4 becomes illegal and to maintain a threat to the WP, Black must play BK–›c3. We have now reached the position shown in Figure 6.7.

4. nearp: The black king is nearer the pawn than the white king.
5. psquare *: The black king can move inside the 'pawn's square'.
6. rp1: The pattern shown in Figure 6.7.
7. rp2 *: The black king can trap the white king on the edge of the board.
8. imcap *: Black can immediately capture the pawn.
9. near2p *: Essentially the pattern shown in Figure 6.8.
10. stalemate *: Positions which lead to stalemate.

The machine-generated decision rule is shown in Figure 6.9.

No. of examples in final working-set = 20.
No. of nodes in final tree = 20.
Time taken to generate rule = 0.84 CPU second.

```
rookpawn_relevant
  t: imcap
    f: rp1
      f: rp2
        f: nearc8
          f: psquare
            t: neara8
              f: nearp
                f: near2p
                  f: stalemate
                    f: TRUE
                    t: FALSE
                  t: FALSE
                t: FALSE
              t: FALSE
            f: TRUE
          t: FALSE
        t: FALSE
      t: TRUE
    t: FALSE
  f: FALSE
```

Figure 6.9 rookpawn decision tree.

6.9 Subproblem 3: get-to-main-pattern

This attribute deals with all positions where main pattern holds or is achievable, the rank of the pawn is less than five, and the pawn is not a rookpawn. There are 31 185 positions in this category, 12 796 of which satisfy the advice. The vast majority of positions were easy to classify with a few hundred proving harder because the pawn is on the second rank, and/or both pieces have to move to achieve main pattern.

The final attribute set was:

1. mainpatt_relevant: Pawn is not on rook's file and pawn rank <= 5.
2. imcap *: The black king can take the pawn immediately.
3. nearerx: The black king can get ahead of the white pawn, disallowing mainpatt.
4. diropb *: The black king has the opposition and the white king is not more than 1 rank ahead of the pawn.
5. diropw *: The white king is one rank ahead of the pawn and has the opposition.
6. anyop *: White has the distant opposition and can get ahead of the pawn.
7. mp1 *: Moving the white king alone White can get to mainpatt 1 rank ahead of the pawn.
8. mp2 *: Moving the white king alone White can get to mainpatt 2 ranks ahead of the pawn.
9. pmove: By first moving the pawn White can get to mainpatt.

The machine-generated decision rule is shown in Figure 6.10.

No. of examples in final working-set = 7.
No. of nodes in final tree = 13.
Time taken to generate rule = 0.28 CPU second.

```
mainpatt_relevant
  t: imcap
    f: pmove
      f: mp1
        f: mp2
          f: diropw
            f: FALSE
            t: TRUE
          t: TRUE
        t: TRUE
      t: TRUE
    t: FALSE
  f: FALSE
```

Figure 6.10 main-pattern decision tree.

6.10 Subproblem 4: rank56

Rank56 holds in any position where the pawn's rank is 5 or 6, it is not a rookpawn, and either mainpatt or r6patt holds or is achievable.

This problem was easy compared with the previous examples since no special cases arose due to the edge of the board or the pawn's initial double move. There are 21 012 legal positions of which 9768 satisfy rank56.

The final attribute set was:

1. rank56_relevant: Pawn is not on rook's file and is on rank 5 or 6.
2. dirop56: The sixth rank pattern holds or can be achieved.
3. btop1 *: The black king is or can get directly in front of the pawn.
4. mp56 *: By moving the king alone White can get to main-pattern.
5. mp1 *: Moving the king alone White can get to main-pattern 1 rank ahead of the pawn.
6. r6patt: Special pattern shown in Figure 6.11.

The machine-generated decision rule is shown in Figure 6.12.

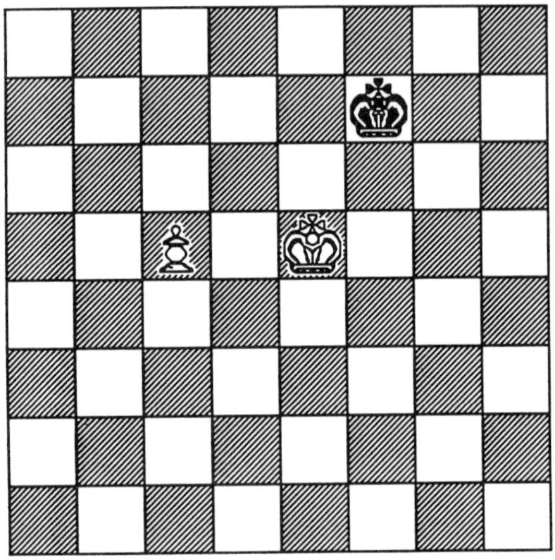

Figure 6.11 Can White take the opposition from Black? (r6patt). Here BK–›e7 (opposition) is answered by WP–›c6. Then after BK–›d8 or BK–›e8, White can take the opposition.

No. of examples in final working-set = 7.
No. of nodes in final tree = 13.
Time taken to generate rule = 0.38 CPU second.

```
rank56_relevant
  t: mp56
    f: dirop56
      f: btop1
        t: mp1
          f: r6patt
            f: FALSE
            t: TRUE
          t: TRUE
        f: TRUE
      t: TRUE
    t: TRUE
  f: FALSE
```

Figure 6.12 rank56 decision tree.

6.11 Subproblem 5: rank7

This was the simplest subproblem. rank7 holds if the pawn is on the seventh rank, canrun is false, the pawn is not on the rook's file and the white king can force its way next to the pawn. Of the 10 506 legal rank7 positions 237 satisfy these conditions. The only difficulty encountered was that three positions that logically ought to satisfy rank7, result in stalemate due to edge conditions. An extra attribute was added to cope with them.

The final attribute set was:

1. rank7_relevant: Pawn is not on rook's file and is on rank 7.

No. of examples in final working-set = 3.
No. of nodes in final tree = 7.
Time taken to generate rule = 0.20 CPU second.

```
rank7_relevant
  t: nxtop
    t: stale
      f: TRUE
      t: FALSE
    f: FALSE
  f: FALSE
```

Figure 6.13 rank7 decision tree.

2. nxtop *: The white king can force its way next to the pawn.
3. stale *: Initial stalemate condition.

The machine-generated decision rule is shown in Figure 6.13.

6.12 Top-level solution for KPK

At this point our use of Quinlan's ID3 moves to a higher level in which we treat the previously synthesized decision trees as primitive attributes. Quinlan's ID3 can then be applied again to form a decision tree in terms of these **sub-trees**.

Although it has been proved that a combination of these subproblems is sufficient to determine the value of any position for WTM, this turns out not to be the case for BTM positions. There is a small class of positions for which an extra attribute must be added. Consider the position shown in Figure 6.14. To deal with this an extra attribute called interfere was added to detect patterns like that shown in this figure.

Figure 6.14 Interference between attributes – a case study. In this position with BTM Black can prevent White forcing mainpattern by BK:h6, and canrun by BK:g6, BK:g7 or BK:g8. Black cannot prevent *both* of these however, and this situation is precisely where the attributes given by the six decision rules for the subproblems are inadequate.

No. of examples in final working-set = 9.
No. of nodes in final rule = 13.
Time taken to generate rule = 0.30 CPU second.

```
canrun
  f: mainpatt
    f: rookpawn
      f: rank56
        f: rank7
          f: interfere
            f: DRAWN
            t: LOST
          t: LOST
        t: LOST
      t: LOST
    t: LOST
  t: LOST
```

Figure 6.15 top-level KPK decision tree.

The attribute set for the complete KPK Black-to-move problem was: ○ canrun, ○ rookpawn, ○ mainpatt, ○ rank56, ○ rank7 and interfere. The first five of these attributes represent the previously synthesized decision trees.

The machine-generated decision rule is shown in Figure 6.15.

6.13 Unstructured induction of decision rule

The final problem we tackled was to produce a decision tree using attributes from all the subproblems, without regard for the imposed top-down structure of the problem. Our intention was to get some idea of the extra complexity introduced, in human terms, by removing our previous structuring of the problem. In addition we would be able to compare the absolute sizes of the two decision trees produced for the full KPK game.

The 34 attributes used were:

- imcap wkahd stlmt ahead plus1 plus2 patt1 crit
  from the CANRUN set of attributes.
- rookpawn_relevant nearc8 neara8 nearp psquare rp1 rp2 near2p stalemate
  from the ROOKPAWN set of attributes.
- mainpatt_relevant nearerx diropb diropw anyop mp1 mp2 pmove
  from the MAINPAT set of attributes.
- rank56_relevant dirop56 btop1 mp56 r6patt
  from the RANK56 set of attributes.

- rank7_relevant nxtop stale
  from the RANK7 set of attributes.

It was also necessary to include interfere. The decision tree generated from these attributes can be found in Appendix A. It should be noted that five attributes (patt1, nearerx, mainpatt_relevant, nxtop and stale) were shown to be unnecessary for this particular unstructured solution. They were left out of the decision tree by Quinlan's ID3. By varying the user-supplied parameters to Quinlan's ID3, i.e. size of the initial working-set, number of contradicting decision-vectors to be added to the working-set with each iteration and the pseudo-random number seed, it was possible to generate a whole series of unstructured decision trees each equivalent in function but omitting different subsets of the above five attributes in the different cases. In all, 128 unstructured trees were generated. The particular unstructured tree detailed in this paper was one of the best (i.e. smallest number of nodes). The user-supplied parameters to Quinlan's ID3 which were discussed earlier did not appear to have any effect on the structured tree. Criteria for the choice of this tree are discussed in Section 6.14.

6.14 Costs associated with decision rules

Inductive synthesis by machine of machine-executable descriptions can be seen as a **manufacturing process**, with the customary categories of cost, efficiency, etc. The analogy can be taken further by likening the databases used to a factory building, the computer to a complex of machine tools and the system programs within the computer to the tool settings. The production side of this manufacturing process can be viewed as the development of attributes (components), the determination of legal decision-vectors (performance and design specification of product) and the synthesis of decision trees (assembly of production prototypes from components). Since both the structured and unstructured trees used the same attributes, the cost of developing attributes for these solutions (pilot R&D) was the same. However, the other two components of this manufacturing cost (decision-vector generation and decision-tree synthesis) merit some discussion. The first of these (the tooling-up cost) is a cost that is independent of the number of decision trees finally produced (all 128 unstructured trees were generated from the one set of decision-vectors). Figure 6.16 shows the figures for decision-vector generation. The measure of computational cost chosen was that of store times time, in kilobyte seconds (kbs for short).

To evaluate the second component of manufacturing cost (decision-tree synthesis) it is necessary to know the size of Quinlan's ID3, the average CPU time to generate an unstructured tree and the total CPU

Problem	Time (CPU seconds)	Size (kbytes) program + database	No. of legal vectors	Cost (kbs)
Structured				
canrun	1760	9.07 + 12.29	51	37 590
rookpawn	543	10.16 + 3.69	69	7 521
mainpat	881	9.14 + 7.37	14	14 545
rank56	665	10.98 + 4.91	11	10 566
rank7	189	9.20 + 2.46	3	2 204
kpk (top-level)	2116	9.27 + 30.72	12	84 619
Total			160	157 045
Unstructured	7252	15.14 + 12.29	1901	198 922

Figure 6.16 Cost of decision-vector generation. Note the cost of generating decision-vectors for the structured solution is the sum of the costs for the six subproblems.

Problem	Time (CPU seconds)	Size (kbytes)	Cost (kbs)
Structured			
canrun	0.60	35.27	21.16
rookpawn	0.84	35.27	29.63
mainpat	0.28	35.27	9.88
rank56	0.38	35.27	13.40
rank7	0.20	35.27	7.05
kpk (top-level)	0.30	35.27	10.60
Total			91.72
Unstructured	140.00	40.62	5686.80

Figure 6.17 Decision-tree synthesis cost. Note the non-linear increase in the cost of generating 'large' decision trees.

time to generate the structured solution. Figure 6.17 shows the relevant figures.

The unstructured solution needed a larger version of Quinlan's ID3 to cope with the extra number of attributes present at one time. This alteration did not add to the tree synthesis time since the structured trees took the same time to generate on the larger Quinlan's ID3. It must be assumed that the discrepancy in tree synthesis cost is a true reflection of the added complexity introduced when generating large unstructured decision trees.

As with other manufacturing exercises the accuracy and efficiency of the manufactured products themselves is also important. To evaluate this factor the decision trees were run and checked for accuracy against a database (Clarke, 1977). All the decision trees generated were 100%

Overhead		
kbytes	seconds	kbs
7.234	15.7	114

Database (program + data) + Overhead		
kbytes	seconds	kbs
8.084 + 12.288 = 20.372	391.7	7979

Structured tree + Overhead + Database evaluation		
kbytes	seconds	kbs
14.884	1984.7	29 540

Unstructured tree + Overhead + Database evaluation (average of 128 trees, working-set increments from 1-1900)		
kbytes	seconds	kbs
15.062	2389	35 983

Unstructured tree + Overhead + Database evaluation (best, working-set increment 250)		
kbytes	seconds	kbs
15.012	1555	23 344

Unstructured tree + Overhead + Database evaluation (worst, working-set increment 1600)		
kbytes	seconds	kbs
15.114	3144	47 518

Figure 6.18 Raw run-time statistics. These statistics were collected on the run-time costs of decision trees and database when used to classify KPK with BTM.

accurate. Because there were so many unstructured trees (128 were tested) the statistics relating to this group is split into three parts; best, average and worst. The same measure of cost (the product of store and processing time in kilobyte seconds) was used. Only one test program was used to determine the execution cost of each decision tree. Many features of this program could be enabled or disabled using a technique of **conditional compilation**. By disabling both the database checking and the tree checking, a measure for the overheads of this program (legal move generation, statistics gathering and evaluation, variable initialization, etc.) could be determined. Subtraction of these values from the raw data yielded the adjusted or true costs. The raw figures are shown in Figure 6.18 and Figure 6.19. The average time to classify a KPK position with BTM is shown in Figure 6.20.

Database		
kbytes	seconds	kbs
13.14	376	4941

Structured tree		
kbytes	seconds	kbs
6.8	1593	10 832

Unstructured tree (average)		
kbytes	seconds	kbs
7.0	1997	13 979

Unstructured tree (best)		
kbytes	seconds	kbs
6.9	1163	8025

Unstructured tree (worst)		
kbytes	seconds	kbs
7.0	2752	19 264

Figure 6.19 Actual cost of classifying all KPK positions with BTM.

Technique	Time (ms)
Database	4.5
Structured tree	19.1
Unstructured tree (average)	23.9
Unstructured tree (best)	13.9
Unstructured tree (worst)	32.9

Figure 6.20 Average time to classify a KPK position with BTM.

6.15 Programmer costs

It took about six man-weeks to complete this portion of the work described. At least half this time was spent considering special cases for the two subproblems rookpawn and get-to-mainpatt. This was due to considerable difficulty found with the iterative refinement of the attributes (steps 3 and 4 in Figure 2.1). When there were only one or two classes of clash the choice of refinement was critical. Changing the definition of an attribute to eliminate one clash caused other clashes with different attributes. This arises when the attributes do not strictly delineate between drawn and won positions over the whole space, but only for the clash being considered. Thus, any change had to be considered for its global effect rather than just locally. It is not clear whether this was due to a bad choice of attributes for the two problems since it did not happen elsewhere, or whether the problems were inherently more difficult. Further experiments should clear this point up.

Despite these problems, total programming time was far faster than with conventional techniques, where the problem can consume several programmer months.

6.16 Structural features of rules

An interesting point that arose from our work on the subproblems is the uniform nature of the decision trees created. Each has one branch with depth one offshoots and this form *also* characterizes the tree synthesized in the final top-level pass (see earlier). This may correspond to the domain expert's conceptualization of the problem. It is certainly very different from the result Quinlan (1979) reports for the KRKN ending, and from the trees synthesized for KPK using unstructured induction.

Another point concerns the ubiquitous 'special cases'. If we eliminate the two attributes patt 1 and stlmt dealing with special cases in the pawn-can-run problem, we produce a 13-node rule (instead of 17) which correctly evaluates 99.998% of the pawn-can-run space. For more complex problems it may be more effective to produce a rule which leaves incorrectly classified a small class of such exceptions, thus keeping the rule within the 'human window' (Michie, 1983a). This could produce compact, humanly accessible rules which people could use successfully in the vast majority of cases, accepting the penalty of having to resolve the remaining cases by other means.

Looking at the manufacturing costs it seems that decision-vector generation for the structured solution is 20% cheaper than for the unstructured solution. For this particular problem this represents a saving of over 40 000 kilobyte seconds. Furthermore, to be reasonably sure of generating an unstructured decision tree that is more cost-effective than the structured tree, several unstructured trees must be sampled, the production cost of each one being over 5000 kbs. Since only 36 of the 128 unstructured solutions were cheaper to run than the structured solution, to achieve a cost-effective result a number of unstructured trees would need to be generated, making the cost of manufacturing a good unstructured solution greater than 40 000 kbs. This is very much more expensive than the structured solution and adds emphasis to the point that adding a humanly understandable structure does not necessarily add to the cost of solving a problem.

Chapter 7

KPa7KR Experiment

7.1 Introduction to the topic

In relation to its complexity the textbook treatment of KPKR is even more sketchy than that of KPK. Indeed the particular subset of KPKR that was chosen for this experiment (WTM WP:a7) is not mentioned at all in any of the books (listed in Appendix B) consulted by the author. This is in line with the conclusion to which the author's investigations have driven him, namely that *the fraction of expert skill which is explicitly accessible (and hence can be codified in books) is a decreasing function of problem-domain complexity*. This conclusion if generally valid would have a bearing on the 'complexity barrier' by which further progress in expert systems work is now confronted.

The original problem decomposition was attempted according to the following rationale.

Since the white pawn is one square away from queening there is only one reason for White not winning, i.e. White is delayed from safely promoting the pawn. Thus the top-down problem decomposition centres on what might be the existing delays to White's promoting the pawn and when such a delay exists can Black capitalize? Due to the good potential mobility of the black rook, Black will either capitalize quickly or not at all. The types of delay that are reflected in the decomposition structure are:

- *Double attack* Delays of this category are encountered when the white king is skewered against the promoted pawn by the black rook or when the black rook forks the white king and promoted pawn. Consider the positions shown in Figure 7.1.
- *Delayed skewer* This type of position can result in a double attack (described above). An example of a 'delayed skewer' is given in Figure 7.2.
- *White king in check* Another potential delay arises when White is in check. Since the white king must move out of check, the black rook may be able to move to the eighth rank or the 'A' file thus preparing to capture the pawn which is threatening to promote. For example see Figure 7.3.

Figure 7.1 Example of a 'double attack' position. If White pushes the pawn to a8 and promotes then Black can move its rook to a2 with check. White has to move his king out of check thereby allowing the black rook to capture the newly promoted white pawn. Complications arise when promoting the pawn puts the black king in check (thus preventing the rook skewer), e.g. with BK:d5. BR:g7 introduces another complication; as the pawn promotes then BR–›a7 can be taken by the promoted WP (Q or R). Further problems arise when the white king is too close to the square on which the black rook is threatening to skewer, e.g. with BR:g4, pawn promotes, BR–›a4, white king can now take the rook. Taking this last variation further with the starting position WK:a5 WQ:a8 BK:b3 BR:g4, the white king is prevented from taking the rook because to do so would place the white king in check. In all of these cases if White does not promote the pawn then the black rook can at worst move to cover the eighth rank which is guaranteed to allow the rook to capture the pawn. This capture may not be safe for Black but it will always result in a not-won-for-White game value.

- *White king on pawn promotion square* When the white king is on the pawn promotion square the delay involved is due to White's having to move this piece before promoting the pawn. If Black can safely attack the promotion square in one move then the value is not-won-for-White. An example of this type of position is given in Figure 7.4.
- *Black is threatening checkmate* The idea here is that if Black is threatening to checkmate White then White must do something about this threat possibly resulting in a delay to promoting the

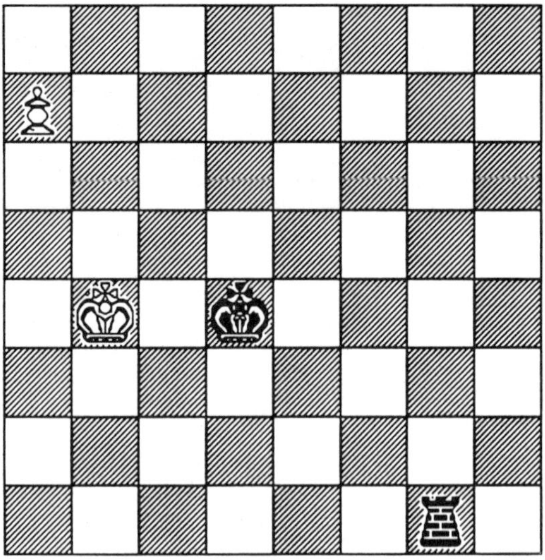

Figure 7.2 Example 'delayed skewer'. If White promotes the pawn then BR–›b1 with check. The white king has to move out of check but is constrained to move leftward because moving to the right would be into check from the black king. On moving to the left (a3, a4 or a5), BR–›a1 (check) results in an immediate skewer. The same type of complications set in as with the immediate skewer except now that two white king moves are involved, the white king distance to the black rook skewering square must be one greater than before, e.g. BR:g2 will not work because WP–›a8, BR–›b2 (check), WK–›a3, now BR–›a2 can be captured by the white king.

pawn. A possible delay of this type that actually does not result in a delay to White's promoting the pawn is illustrated in Figure 7.5.

The complete (100% correct) decision structure comprised nine trees at four different levels, making up 108 nodes in all. This structure was run 15 times on all the legal positions in the KPa7KR WTM domain. The timing results are shown in Figure 7.6.

7.2 Previous computer work

Apart from automatic construction of lookup databases, no computer construction of verifiably correct knowledge systems has previously been recorded on this endgame (with or without restrictions to any one piece), nor indeed on any other endgame of greater complexity.

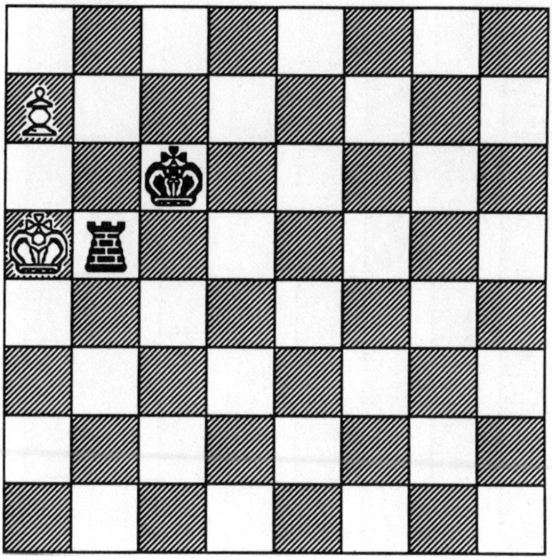

Figure 7.3 Example 'white king in check' delay position. Here the white king is in check and must move out of the way, but is constrained to remain on the 'A' file (a4 or a5) by the rook. The white king cannot take the rook because it is defended by the black king. After the white king has moved the black rook would normally be moved to rank 8 (to guarantee a not-won-for-White value) but in this case the eighth rank square is defended by the white pawn. The BR→a5 move is defended by the white king. In this case BR→b1 introduces a good skewer threat and results in not-won-for-White. Other complications involve multiple check where white king and black rook may walk from one end of the board to the other before a result is obtained.

7.3 Structured induction of decision rule

Since all the examples originated from domain experts it was essential to produce simple decision trees that could readily be understood so that the expert could improve them after inspection by incremental addition of refutation examples. This also meant that the attributes themselves had to be simple. The rules of thumb used to make sure this was the case were, firstly, attributes should not be longer than a screenful of C code and, secondly, subproblems should have solution trees invoking no more than seven attributes. The latter was *strictly* adhered to (none of the solution trees exceeded seven attributes). The former was treated mainly as a guideline. However, when one of the attributes (btoqs in subproblem wkchk) grew to 55 lines of C code it was turned into a subproblem. The process of turning btoqs into a subproblem was semi-automatic as follows:

1. Take all the examples so far supplied by the experts and evaluate

Figure 7.4 An example 'white king on pawn promotion square' position. The white king must move to either b7 or b8. The black rook will be moved to a6 to ensure that the promoting pawn can be captured. However, if the initial white king move is to b7, the WR to a6 move is blocked. Black's answer to this is BR→b6 (check) this forces the white king to a8 or c8 or c7. Whichever of these moves White makes, Black answers with BR to a6 eventually resulting in the capture of the pawn and a not-won-for-White value. In order for this type of complication to work, the black king must defend the BR to b6 move.

the original function (in this case btoqs) storing the result for future use as position/class-value pairs.

2. Inspect the original function code and draw a box around each return point and its associated code.
3. Group the boxes into larger more meaningful boxes and give each of these a name.
4. Invoke Interactive ID3 on these named groups of code using the position/class-value pairs in (1) as training examples.

The use of Interactive ID3 allows for the possibility of a more sensible ordering of code than was present in the original function. Appendix C shows the original btoqs attribute code and the name assignments made by the author. The original 55 lines of C code became 61 lines but of the five attributes chosen, none exceeded 21 lines and the result was a more humanly understandable function.

The average length of hand-coded attributes was about 15 statements of C. Once again, the problem decomposition reflected the domain expert's intuitive feel for the problem's structure. This intuitive

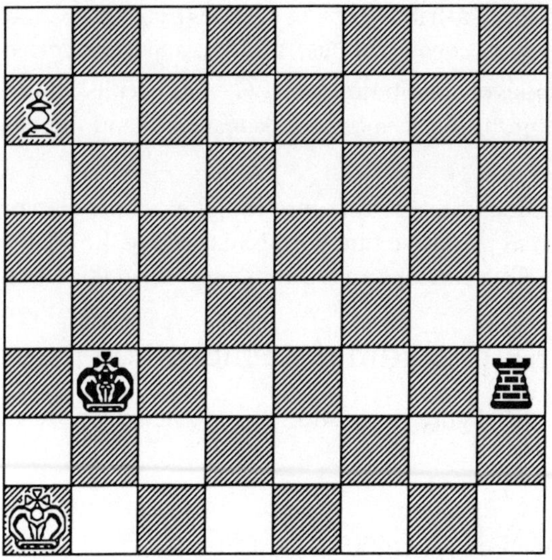

Figure 7.5 A 'threatened checkmate' position. Here the threat is that Black may move his rook to h1 with checkmate. However, if WP–›a8 promotes to a queen, the h1 square is attacked by this piece. If the starting position was with BR:h4 then after WP–›a8, BR–›a4 (check) and then the newly promoted queen must take the BR (WQ–›a4) and BK–›a4 captures the queen, result not-won-for-White (draw).

Cost of classifying all legal (209 718) positions (kbs)	
Mean	29 224.1
Standard deviation	674.1

Figure 7.6 Timing results for the (100% correct) structured decision rule. Mean and standard deviation for 15 runs over all the legal KPa7KR WTM positions.

feel caused a possible anomaly; the subproblem ds (delayed skewer) should probably be housed within dq (good delay to queening) but one of the experts (Dr Kopec) was happier with it being a top-level subproblem.

A full description of the attributes and subproblems follows. Attributes that are marked with * are evaluated using the CLIP/C emulator. Attributes that are marked with ○ are subproblems. The number in brackets after every C-coded attribute is the number of C statements that defines that attribute. There are two exceptions to this measurement:

1. The top-level attribute chkmt (5 lines) calls two other C functions (white_king_in_check (6 lines) and no_white_king_move (3 lines)).
2. The top-level attribute stlmt (1 line) calls three C functions (white_king_in_check, no_white_king_move and no_white_pawn_move (7 lines)).

These other C functions do not figure in the attribute size measurement as they are treated as primitive functions like those of the CLIP emulator (e.g. cand (5 lines)). One-line attributes are of the form return(<expression>).

7.4 KPa7KR problem decomposition tree

Referring to the figure opposite, subproblems are circled, primitive attributes are boxed.

7.5 Subproblem (level 1): pa7

This is the top-level tree for KPKR with WP:a7 and WTM. It was the last tree in the structured set to be generated (due to the requirements of bottom-up implementation). There are 209 718 legal positions classified by pa7, 129 825 are won-for-white while 79 893 are not-won-for-white. Of the six attributes originally chosen by the domain experts for this level only five turned out to be necessary. The one that was left out by Interactive ID3 (chkmt) is functionally subsumed by dq and bxqsq. Some implications of this omission will be discussed later.

Figure 7.7 The 'queening square'. Here the pawn promotion (queening) square (marked) is controlled by the black rook.

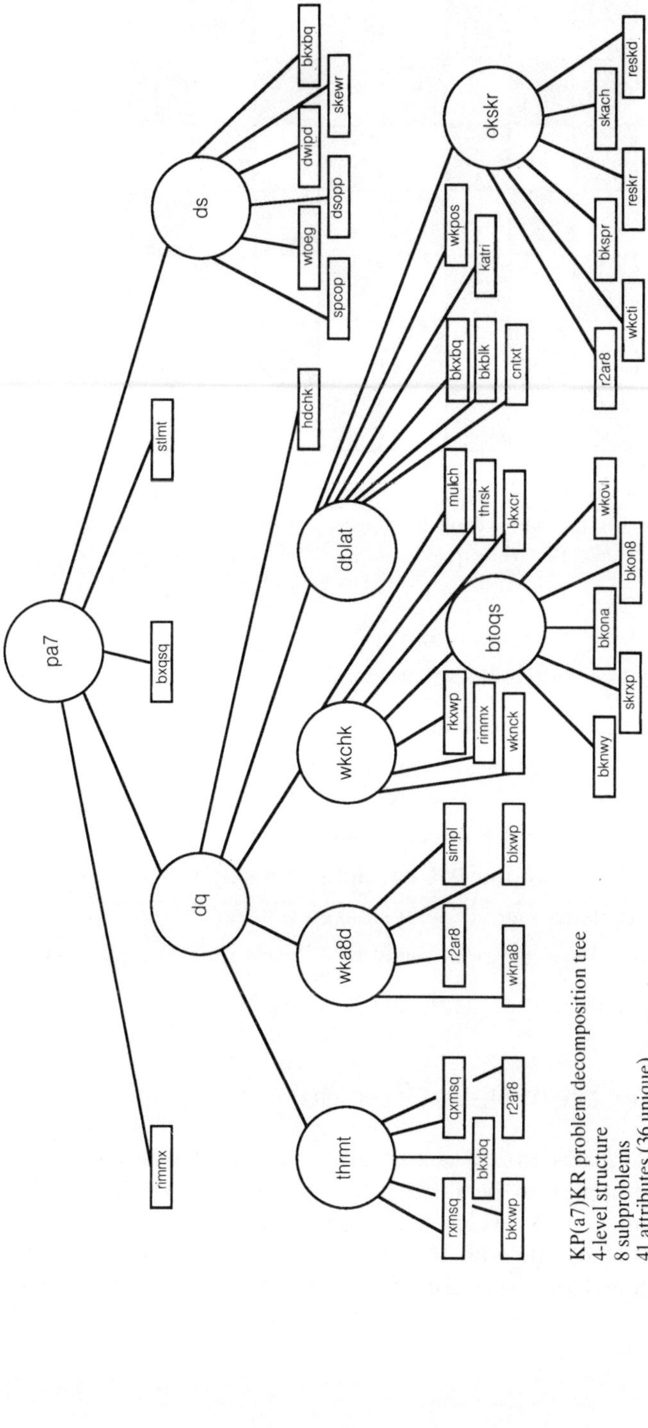

KP(a7)KR problem decomposition tree
4-level structure
8 subproblems
41 attributes (36 unique)
209 718 legal positions (WTM)
129 825 WFW 79 893 not WFW
Information content of structure 84%

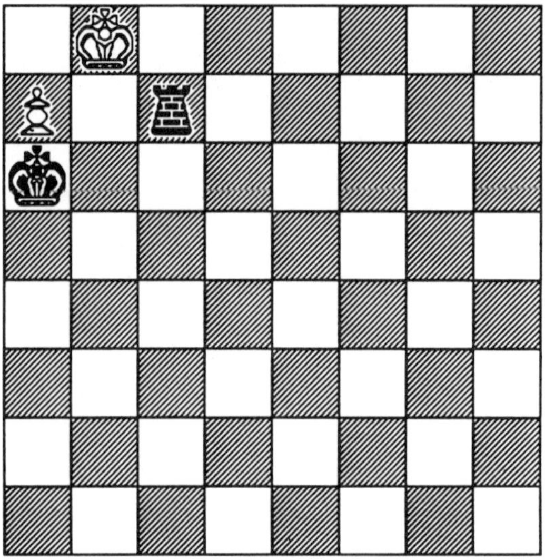

Figure 7.8 Can the BR be captured safely? In this position it would not be considered safe for the white king to capture the black rook because the black king would then take the white pawn.

The final pa7 attribute set was:

1. chkmt (5)*: Is the WK in checkmate.
2. bxqsq (6)*: Does one or more black piece control the queening square. The 'queening square' is shown in Figure 7.7.
3. stlmt (1)*: Is the WK in stalemate.
4. rimmx (15)*: Can the BR be captured safely (see Figure 7.8).
5. ds ○: Is there a good delayed skewer threat.
6. dq ○: Is there a simple delay to White's queening the pawn.

The machine-generated decision rule is shown in Figure 7.9.

7.6 Subproblem (level 2.1): dq

This subproblem acts mostly as a sequencer for attributes that the expert thought too complex to be dealt with immediately. There is only one simple attribute (hdchk) which deals with problems caused by the black king moving out of line with the black rook allowing the black rook to check the white king. The rest of the attributes are subproblems that decide whether there is a delay to White's promoting the pawn that Black can successfully capitalize on.

No. of examples in final working-set = 6.
No. of nodes in final rule = 11.
Time taken to generate rule = 0.12 CPU second.

```
rimmx
  f: dq
    f: bxqsq
      f: stlmt
        f: ds
          f: WON
          t: NOT
        t: NOT
      t: NOT
    t: NOT
  t: WON
```

Run-time behaviour for each test		
Test	Number decided	Leaving
rimmx	21 391 (WON)	188 327 undecided
dq	43 663 (NOT)	144 664 undecided
bxqsq	36 081 (NOT)	108 583 undecided
stlmt	48 (NOT)	108 535 undecided
ds	101 (NOT)	108 434 (WON)

Figure 7.9 pa7 (top-level) decision tree.

Of the 188 327 positions that reach this far in the structured hierarchy 43 663 classify true and 144 664 classify false. In other words 43 663 positions are not-won-for-White because of a delay to pawn promotion dealt with by this subproblem.

The final dq attribute set was:

1. thrmt ○: Is there a good delay for Black to White's promoting the pawn because there is a mate threat.
2. wka8d ○: Is there a good delay for Black to White's promoting the pawn because the white king is on square a8.
3. wkchk ○: Is there a good delay for Black to White's promoting the pawn because the white king is in check.
4. dblat ○: Is there a good delay for Black to White's promoting the pawn because of a double attack threat.
5. hdchk (12)*: Is there a good delay for Black to White's promoting the pawn because there is a hidden check (see Figure 7.10).

The machine-generated decision rule is shown in Figure 7.11.

Figure 7.10 A 'hidden check'. If WP–›a8 then BK–›b[2–3] which is a good immediate skewer and not-won-for-White. If White does not promote the pawn then Black makes the same move and threatens to take the pawn (a move that will still result in a not-won-for-White value).

7.7 Subproblem (level 2.2): ds

As described above, this problem deals with whether the threat of a delayed skewer prevents White from promoting the pawn and results in a not-won-for-White result. Of the 108 535 positions to pass through this subproblem, 101 classify true and 108 434 classify false.

The final ds attribute set was:

1. wtoeg (6)*: Is the white king one away from the relevant edge. The relevant edge is defined to be the edge that the black rook will eventually use to attack the white king and promoted pawn.
2. dsopp (1)*: Are the kings in normal opposition. Normal opposition exists when the two kings are separated by one empty square in a line perpendicular to the 'relevant edge' with the black king closer to the centre of the board than the white king (see Figure 7.12).
3. dwipd (3)*: Is the white king distance to intersect point too great. The intersect point is the square that the black rook will use on the

No. of examples in final working-set = 6.
No. of nodes in final rule = 11.
Time taken to generate rule = 0.12 CPU second.

```
thrmt
  f: wka8d
    f: wkchk
      f: dblat
        f: hdchk
          f: FALSE
          t: TRUE
        t: TRUE
      t: TRUE
    t: TRUE
  t: TRUE
```

Run-time behaviour for each test		
Test	Number decided	Leaving
thrmt	821 (TRUE)	187 506 undecided
wka8d	3 152 (TRUE)	184 354 undecided
wkchk	32 698 (TRUE)	151 656 undecided
dblat	6 962 (TRUE)	144 694 undecided
hdchk	30 (TRUE)	144 664 (FALSE)

Figure 7.11 dq decision tree.

'relevant edge'. This attribute tests whether or not the white king will be able to attack that square thus preventing the final skewer.

4. skewr (5)*: Is there a potential skewer as opposed to fork. This attribute determines whether the intersect point is between the promoted pawn and the white king or not. If it is between (fork) then the final check at the intersect point will not work since the newly promoted pawn will simply take the black rook. The only way for a fork to work is if the intersect point is defended by the black king. This cannot be true within ds because of the king opposition requirements (the black king cannot both be in opposition with the white king and defend the intersect point).
5. bkxbq (1)*: Is the black king attacked in some way by the promoted white pawn.
6. spcop (1)*: Is there a special opposition pattern present (see Figure 7.13).

The machine-generated decision rule is shown in Figure 7.14.

Figure 7.12 Normal opposition.

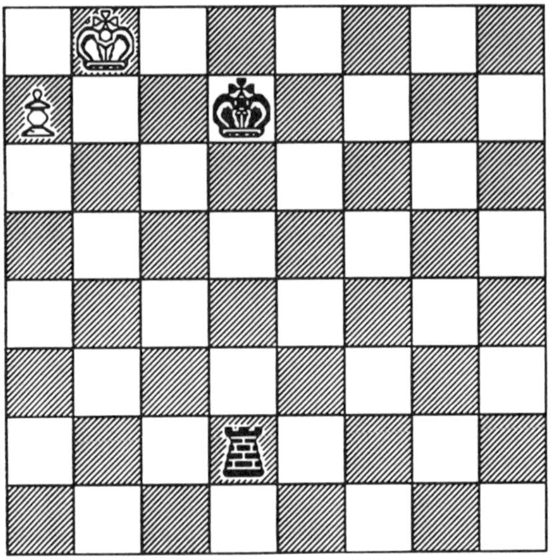

Figure 7.13 Special opposition. Here normal opposition is not present but due to the white king being on an edge, the only move that allows escape from check (after pawn promotion and BR–›b2) is WK–›a7. Now BR–›b1 is a skewer.

No. of examples in final working-set = 7.
No. of nodes in final rule = 13.
Time taken to generate rule = 0.31 CPU second.

```
spcop
  f: wtoeg
    t: dsopp
      t:dwipd
        t: skewr
          t: bkxbq
            f: TRUE
            t: FALSE
          f: FALSE
        f: FALSE
      f: FALSE
    f: FALSE
  t: TRUE
```

Run-time behaviour for each test		
Test	Number decided	Leaving
spcop	5 (TRUE)	108 530 undecided
wtoeg	84 783 (FALSE)	23 747 undecided
dsopp	23 182 (FALSE)	565 undecided
dwipd	325 (FALSE)	240 undecided
skewr	120 (FALSE)	120 undecided
bkxbq	24 (FALSE)	96 (TRUE)

Figure 7.14 ds decision tree.

7.8 Subproblem (level 3.1): thrmt

As described above, this problem deals with whether the threat of checkmate prevents White from promoting the pawn and results in a not-won-for-White result. Of the 188 327 positions to pass through this subproblem, 821 classify true and 187 506 classify false.

The final thrmt attribute set was:

1. rxmsq (41)*: Does the black rook attack a mating square safely. The mating square is the square that the black rook will use to checkmate the white king. This attribute also makes sure that there is a mating square in the first place.
2. bkxbq (1)*: Is the black king attacked in some way by the promoted white pawn.
3. qxmsq (1)*: Is the mating square attacked in some way by the promoted white pawn.

4. r2ar8 (31)*: Does the black rook have safe access to file A or rank 8. If it does then if there is a delay to promoting the white pawn, Black can move the rook to the safe square on rank 8 or file A and always capture the pawn next move. This will always result in a not-won-for-White game value (but not necessarily a won-for-Black game value).
5. bkxwp (1)*: Can the black king attack the white pawn. If it can then the mate threat has prevented White moving the pawn out of the way (because White had to move its king out of check) thus resulting in the safe capture (for Black) of the pawn.

The machine-generated decision rule is shown in Figure 7.15.

No. of examples in final working-set = 6.
No. of nodes in final rule = 11.
Time taken to generate rule = 0.27 CPU second.

```
rxmsq
  t: bkxwp
    f: bkxbq
      f: qxmsq
        f: r2ar8
          f: FALSE
          t: TRUE
        t: FALSE
      t: FALSE
    t: TRUE
  f: FALSE
```

Run-time behaviour for each test		
Test	Number decided	Leaving
rxmsq	186 691 (FALSE)	1636 undecided
bkxwp	136 (TRUE)	1500 undecided
bkxbq	250 (FALSE)	1250 undecided
qxmsq	556 (FALSE)	694 undecided
r2ar8	685 (TRUE)	9 (FALSE)

Figure 7.15 thrmt decision tree.

7.9 Subproblem (level 3.2): wka8d

As described above, this problem deals with delays to the promotion of the pawn because the white king is on the promotion square. If Black can make use of this delay the value of the subproblem is true and the top-level tree will return the result not-won-for-White. Of the 187 506 positions to pass through this subproblem, 3152 classify true and 184 354 classify false.

The final wka8d attribute set was:

1. r2ar8 (31)*: Does the black rook have safe access to file A or rank 8.
2. wkna8 (1)*: Is the white king on square a8.
3. blxwp (2)*: Does Black attack the white pawn (black rook in direction $x < 0$, $y = 0$ only).
4. dblch (9)*: Can the white king be checked away from safety (see Figure 7.16).
5. simpl (5): Does a very simple pattern apply. Deals with a stalemate (WK:a8 WP:a7 BK:a5 BR:b5), a delayed skewer (WK:a8 WP:a7 BK:d8 BR:d6) and a perpetual check (WK:a8 WP:a7 BK:a5 BR:c5). This is the only non-CLIP attribute in the KPKR solution, its code is given in Figure 7.17 to indicate how difficult to understand a simple *non-CLIP* chess-pattern match can be.

The machine-generated decision rule is shown in Figure 7.18.

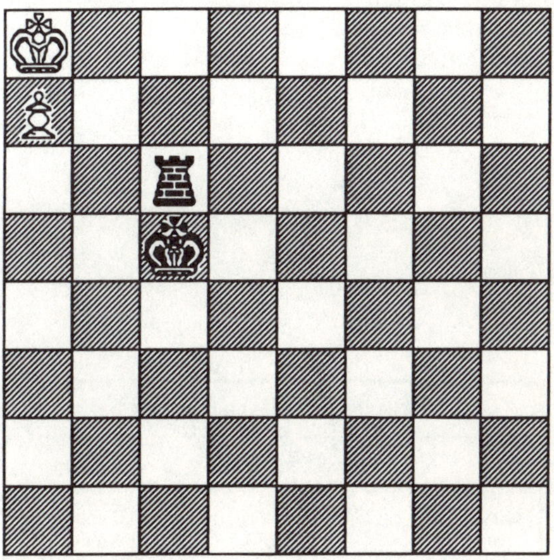

Figure 7.16 Can the white king be checked away from safety? Here WK→b7 is forced (prevents r2ar8) but BR→b6 (check) forces the white king to either retreat to a8 or c8 where BR→a6 makes sure of a not-won-for-White value. This attribute was found by Interactive ID3 to be unnecessary.

```
simpl() {
  if((bf == rf && rf == 4) || (br == rr && rr == 5))
    return(comment(TRUE, FALSE, "", "", "", LEVEL));
  if((bf == rf && != 7) || (br == rr && bf != 2)) {
    return(comment(!(rr == 6 && rf == 3 && (br == rr && bf > 4) ||
       (bf == rf && br < = 4)), FALSE, "", "", "", LEVEL));
  }
  return(comment(FALSE, FALSE, "", "", "", LEVEL));
}
```

Figure 7.17 A simpl definition.

7.10 Subproblem (level 3.3): wkchk

As previously described, this problem deals with delays to the promotion of the pawn because the white king is in check. If Black can make use of this delay the value of the subproblem is true and the top-level tree will return the result not-won-for-White. Of the 184 354 positions to pass through this subproblem, 32 698 classify true and 151 656 classify false. The call to the rimmx attribute is completely redundant in this

No. of examples in final working-set = 5.
No. of nodes in final rule = 9.
Time taken to generate rule = 0.23 CPU second.

```
wkna8
  t: r2ar8
    f: blxwp
      f: simpl
        f: FALSE
        t: TRUE
      t: TRUE
    t: TRUE
  f: FALSE
```

Run-time behaviour for each test		
Test	Number decided	Leaving
wkna8	184 153 (FALSE)	3353 undecided
r2ar8	3 055 (TRUE)	298 undecided
blxwp	63 (TRUE)	235 undecided
simpl	34 (TRUE)	201 (FALSE)

Figure 7.18 wka8d decision tree.

Figure 7.19 Is there a skewer threat lurking? Here the white king must move out of check and can move to one of four squares (a2, a4, b2 or c2) but there are two main features of this position as follows:

- WK–›a4, BR–›d1 now if WP–›a8 (promotes) then BR–›a1 (skewer).
- WK–›a2, BR–›d2 (check). If WK–›c2 to threaten to capture the black rook then BR–›a2 and will capture the white pawn next move. In fact this theme works for any white king move except WK–›a4, i.e. keep checking the white king with the rook along d[1–3]. If the white king strays into the C file then BR–›a? will win the pawn. The white king will eventually have to move to a4 or draw by repetition. Either way is not-won-for-White.

subproblem. No positions are classified as a result of applying that test in this subproblem. This situation arises because if the subproblem is taken in isolation, the question of the rook's safe capture is very important. However, *no* positions where the black rook can be safely captured actually reach this subproblem because they have been filtered out by the call to rimmx in the top-level tree.

The final wkchk attribute set was:

1. btoqs ○: Can Black attack the queening square soon. This was a 55 line attribute; it was turned into a subproblem as described at the beginning of this chapter (Section 7.3).
2. wknck (6)*: Is the white king in check.
3. rimmx (15)*: Can the black rook be captured safely.
4. bkxcr (3)*: Can the black king attack the critical square (b7).
5. rkxwp (2)*: Does the black rook bear on the WP (direction $x < 0$, $y = 0$ only).

6. thrsk (31)*: Is there a skewer threat lurking (see Figure 7.19).
7. mulch (18)*: Can Black renew the check to good advantage (see Figure 7.20).

The machine-generated decision rule is shown in Figure 7.22.

7.11 Subproblem (level 3.4): dblat

This subproblem deals with delays to the promotion of the pawn by reason of double attack. If Black can make use of this delay the value of the subproblem is true and the top-level tree will return the result not-won-for-White. This subproblem fell foul of the number-of-attributes-per-tree criterion but was very easy to split into two subproblems; the first (dblat) establishes context for a double attack, the second (okskr) decides whether or not Black can make use of the potential delay. A successful double attack usually involves a skewer but it can also involve a fork where the black king supports the black rook (see Figure 7.22).

Of the 151 656 positions to pass through this subproblem, 6962 classify true and 144 694 classify false.

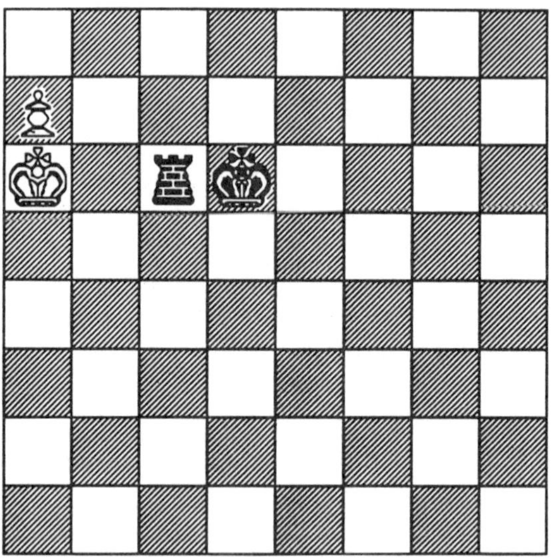

Figure 7.20 Can Black renew the check to good advantage? Here the white king must move to b7 to prevent BR→c8 or BR→a6. But BR→c7 (check) ensures a not-won-for-White value because the white king must now move out of check exposing the white pawn to the black rook.

No. of examples in final working-set = 8.
No. of nodes in final rule = 15.
Time taken to generate rule = 0.50 CPU second.

```
wknck
  t: rimmx
    f: rkxwp
      f: btoqs
        f: bkxcr
          f: thrsk
            f: mulch
              f: FALSE
              t: TRUE
            t: TRUE
          t: TRUE
        t: TRUE
      t: TRUE
    t: FALSE
  f: FALSE
```

Run-time behaviour for each test		
Test	Number decided	Leaving
wknck	150 292 (FALSE)	34 062 undecided
rimmx	0 (FALSE)	34 062 undecided
rkxwp	3 348 (TRUE)	30 714 undecided
btoqs	27 677 (TRUE)	3 047 undecided
bkxcr	1 057 (TRUE)	1 990 undecided
thrsk	64 (TRUE)	1 926 undecided
mulch	552 (TRUE)	1 364 (FALSE)

Figure 7.21 wkchk decision tree. Note the rimmx test does not contribute towards the classification of any positions. It has already been called in the top-level (pa7) subtree so no positions with rimmx = TRUE reach this part of the tree. The reason that this test is included is because this subproblem was induced in isolation of the rest of the solution hierarchy. Thus rook-immediate-capture is an important feature but, for this particular solution, it has already been tested.

The final dblat attribute set was:

1. cntxt (1)*: Is the white king on an edge and not on a8.
2. katri (13)*: Does any king control intersect point. If so, which? This is the only three valued attribute in the KPa7KR WTM solution. If any one king controls the square that the black rook is going to use to skewer White's pieces then that king's side will prevail. If both or neither king controls this square then further information is needed.

3. bkblk (6)*: Is the black king in the way of the black rook.
4. wkpos (3)*: Is the white king in a potential fork position as opposed to a skewer position, i.e. is the black rook intersection point in between White's pieces or not.
5. bkxbq (1)*: Is the black king attacked in some way by the promoted white pawn.
6. okskr o: Can Black take advantage of this potential skewer.

The machine-generated decision rule is shown in Figure 7.23.

7.12 Subproblem (level 4.1): okskr

This subproblem deals with whether a potential skewer is of value to Black. It is called from the dblat subproblem (described above). If this subproblem returns true then dblat and dq will return true and the top-level tree will return the result not-won-for-White. Of the 6584 positions to pass through this subproblem, 6094 classify true and 490 classify false.

Figure 7.22 A supported fork. Here, if WP–›a8 (promotes) then BR–›a4 (check), the white king must move out of check or the promoted pawn (queen or rook) must take the black rook. If the former then the black rook takes the newly promoted pawn (not-won-for-White). If the latter then the black king takes the white queen or rook (not-won-for-White). If the white pawn does not promote then the black rook can get to file A or rank 8 (again not-won-for-White).

No. of examples in final working-set = 12.
No. of nodes in final rule = 14.
Time taken to generate rule = 0.55 CPU second.

```
cntxt
  t: bkblk
    f: bkxbq
      f: katri
        N: wkpos
          f: okskr
            f: FALSE
            t: TRUE
          t: FALSE
        B: TRUE
        W: FALSE
      t: FALSE
    t: FALSE
  f: FALSE
```

Run-time behaviour for each test		
Test	Number decided	Leaving
cntxt	117 052 (FALSE)	34 604 undecided
bkblk	3 425 (FALSE)	31 179 undecided
bkxbq	7 783 (FALSE)	23 396 undecided
katri	868 (TRUE)	
	5 476 (FALSE)	17 052 undecided
wkpos	10 468 (FALSE)	6 584 undecided
okskr	6 094 (TRUE)	490 (FALSE)

Figure 7.23 dblat decision tree.

The final okskr attribute set was:

1. r2ar8 (31)*: Does the black rook have safe access to file A or rank 8.
2. wkcti (33)*: Can the white king control the intersect point. The intersect point is the square on an edge that the black rook will use to skewer White.
3. bkspr (6)*: Can the black king support the black rook. This matters in the case of a 'fork' type double attack where the black rook will end up between the white king and pawn.
4. reskr (14)*: Can the black rook alone renew the double attack threat (see Figure 7.24).
5. skach (10)*: Can the white king be skewered after one or more checks (see Figure 7.25).

Figure 7.24 Can the black rook alone renew the double attack threat? In this position WK–›a5 prevents BR–›a4 (skewer), but BR–›b1 again threatens to skewer on a1 after the next White move. White cannot prevent this hence the term 'renewed skewer'.

Figure 7.25 Can the white king be skewered after one or more checks? Here WK–›a2 is forced to prevent BR–›a1 (skewer). BR–›b2 (check) is the reply, now if WK–›a1 then BR–›b1 (check), WK–›a2, BR–›b2 (check). Eventually the white king is forced to move to a3 or draw by repetition. When this move is made then BR–›b1 is back to the original position. Again either draw by repetition or WK–›a4 in which case BR–›a1 (skewer). In all cases the value is not-won-for-White.

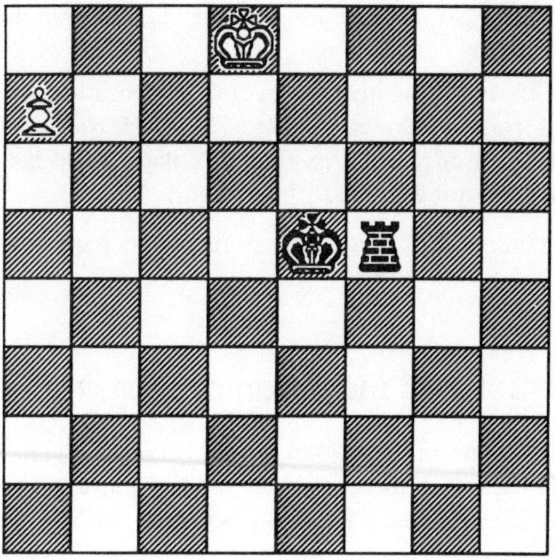

Figure 7.26 Can the white king be reskewered via a delayed skewer? In this position WK–›e7 prevents BR–›f8 which would prevent the white pawn promoting and eventually lead to pawn capture. After WK–›e7 then BR–›h5 threatens BR–›h8 next move. WP–›a8 (promote to queen) prevents the BR–›h8 move but Black replies with BR–›h7 (check). This is now a delayed skewer of the kind previously described.

6. reskd (7)*: Can the white king be reskewered via a delayed skewer (see Figure 7.26).

The machine-generated decision rule is shown in Figure 7.27.

7.13 Subproblem (level 4.2): btoqs

This subproblem deals with whether Black can get to the promotion square and make use of a delay caused by the white king being in check. It is called from the wkchk subproblem. Of the 30 714 positions to pass through this subproblem, 27 677 classify true and 3037 classify false.

The final btoqs attribute set was:

1. skrxp (7)*: Can the black rook achieve a skewer or black king attack the white pawn (see Figure 7.28).
2. bkona (21)*: Is the black king on file A in a position to aid the black rook (see Figure 7.29).
3. bkon8 (13)*: Is the black king on rank 8 in a position to aid the black rook. The same kind of position as bkona but with the black king on rank 8.

4. bknwy (11)*: Is the black king in the black rook's way (see Figure 7.30).
5. wkovl (9)*: Is the white king overloaded and not able to cover all the black rook's intersect points. The black rook's intersect points are those safe edge squares that the black rook can use to attack the pawn promotion square (see Figure 7.31).

The machine-generated decision rule is shown in Figure 7.32.

7.14 Unstructured induction of decision rule

As with the KPK experiment, unstructured trees were generated from the base-level attributes and the entire set of decision-vectors: 3196 vectors result from the 209 718 legal KPa7KR positions with WTM.

No. of examples in final working-set = 7.
No. of nodes in final rule = 13.
Time taken to generate rule = 0.42 CPU second.

```
r2ar8
  f: wkcti
    t: bkspr
      f: reskr
        f: skach
          f: reskd
            f: FALSE
            t: TRUE
          t: TRUE
        t: TRUE
      t: TRUE
    f: TRUE
  t: TRUE
```

Run-time behaviour for each test		
Test	Number decided	Leaving
r2ar8	5956 (TRUE)	628 undecided
wkcti	31 (TRUE)	597 undecided
bkspr	4 (TRUE)	593 undecided
reskr	73 (TRUE)	520 undecided
skach	6 (TRUE)	514 undecided
reskd	24 (TRUE)	490 (FALSE)

Figure 7.27 okskr decision tree.

Figure 7.28 Can the BR achieve a skewer or BK attack the WP? In this position WK–›a2 is forced (to prevent BR–›a3) but BR–›b4 renews the threat for the black rook to get to the A file. Now whatever White does (even if White promotes the pawn) then BR–›a4 (fork type double attack supported by the black king).

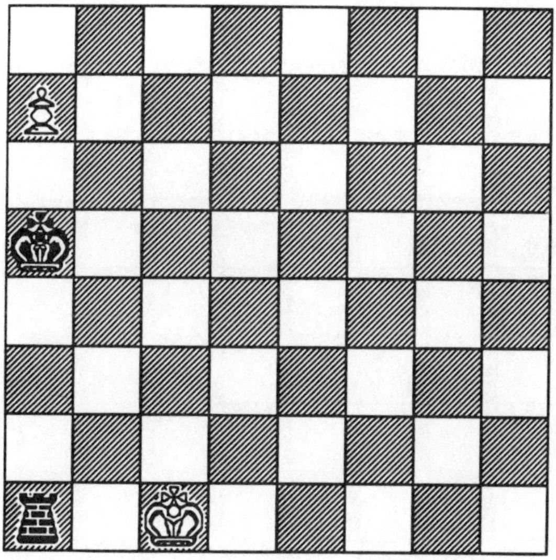

Figure 7.29 Is the BK on file A in a position to aid the BR? Here WK–›b2 attacks the black rook. The black king is too far away to aid the black rook however BK–›b6 threatens to capture the pawn if the white king takes the black rook. WP–›a8 (promotes) is White's only escape from pawn capture, however, the black rook can now take the newly promoted pawn.

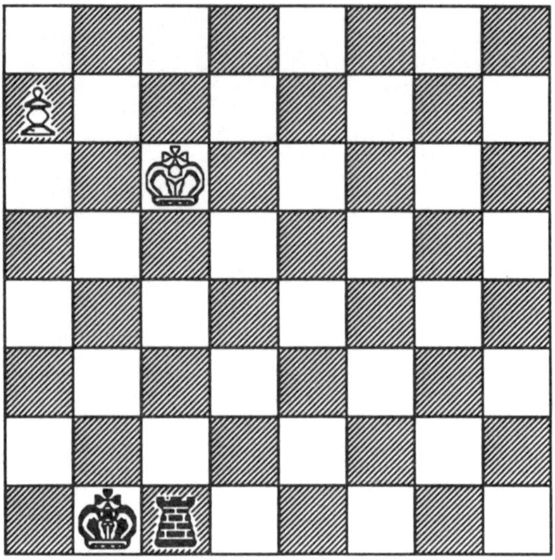

Figure 7.30 Is the black king in the black rook's way? In this position WK–›b7 prevents BR–›c8. Black would normally be able to move the black rook to a1 but the black king is in the way.

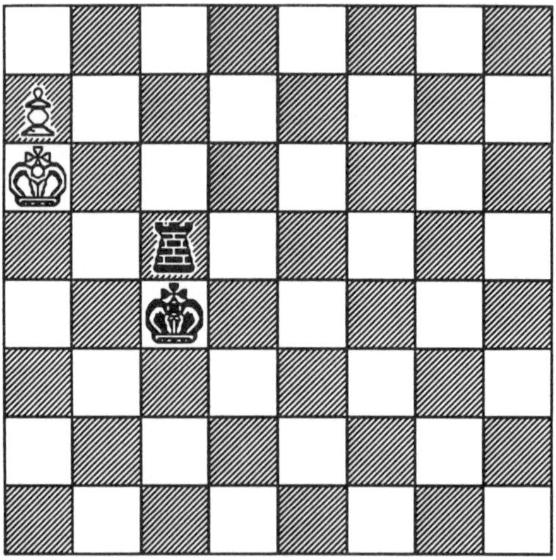

Figure 7.31 Is the white king overloaded? In this position WK–›b6 prevents BR–›a5 but cannot prevent BR–›c8 and eventual capture of the white pawn.

No. of examples in final working-set = 6.
No. of nodes in final rule = 11.
Time taken to generate rule = 0.23 CPU second.

```
bknwy
  f: skrxp
    f: bkona
      f: bkon8
        f: wkovl
          f: FALSE
          t: TRUE
        t: TRUE
      t: TRUE
    t: TRUE
  t: FALSE
```

Run-time behaviour for each test		
Test	Number decided	Leaving
bknwy	434 (FALSE)	30 280 undecided
skrxp	998 (TRUE)	29 282 undecided
bkona	291 (TRUE)	28 991 undecided
bkon8	155 (TRUE)	28 836 undecided
wkovl	26 233 (TRUE)	2 603 (FALSE)

Figure 7.32 btoqs decision tree.

The 36 attributes used were:

- bxqsq stlmt rimmx
  from the PA7 (top level) set of attributes.
- hdchk
  from the DQ set of attributes.
- wtoeg dsopp dwipd skewr bkxbq spcop
  from the DS set of attributes.
- rxmsq r2ar8 bkxwp
  from the THRMT set of attributes.
- wkna8 blxwp dblch simpl
  from the WKA8D set of attributes.
- wknck bkxcr rkxwp thrsk mulch
  from the WKCHK set of attributes.
- cntxt katri bkblk wkpos
  from the DBLAT set of attributes.

- wkcti bkspr reskr skach reskd
  from the OKSKR set of attributes.
- skrxp bkona bkon8 bknwy wkovl
  from the BTOQS set of attributes.

By again varying the user-supplied parameters to Quinlan's ID3 another series of trees (50 in all) was generated, each equivalent to the structured tree in function though not in understandability. Appendix D shows the best (smallest) unstructured tree generated in this manner. The rules were run over the entire set of legal KPa7KR WTM positions and the statistics shown in Figure 7.33 were gathered.

	Cost of classifying all legal (209 718) positions (kbs)	Number of nodes
Mean	24 768.1	95.6
Standard deviation	2 720.0	7.9

Figure 7.33 Vital statistics for 50 (100% correct) unstructured trees. Each rule was run once over all the legal KPa7KR WTM positions.

7.15 Generation of unstructured decision rules using structured training set

Of the 3196 legal decision-vectors only 61 were necessary (minimal or near-minimal reconstruction set) to generate the structured solution (corresponding to 61 examples supplied at different levels in the decomposition hierarchy). About 170 were needed to generate the unstructured solutions. In the context of the structured decomposition hierarchy the 61 decision-vectors are sufficient to specify the KPa7KR WTM problem completely. However, removed from this context these vectors are not sufficient to classify the problem completely. It could be said that the decompositions hierarchy is worth about 110 examples in this case.

Another way to look at the value of the decomposition hierarchy is to find out what percentage of positions are incorrectly classified by decision trees trained from these 61 vectors: 66 unstructured trees were generated using the structured training set of 61 examples. Each tree was tested against the database for accuracy. The results are shown in Figure 7.34. Note that the observed error rate of about 30% represents very poor reliability, since a random classifier (knowing only the frequency of won positions in the domain) would have about a 38% error rate. Implications are further discussed in Section 8.3.

	% correct	Cost of classifying all legal (209 718) positions (kbs)	Number of nodes
Mean	72.1	14 604.5	153.73
Standard deviation	5.2	1 003.7	9.10

Figure 7.34 Statistics for 66 unstructured trees trained using structured training set. These decision trees were trained using only the 61 decision-vectors that were used to induce the structured solution. The number of examples necessary to generate completely correct unstructured trees in the absence of expert supplied structure was 175 in one experiment.

7.16 Discussion of results

First a word on the accuracy of timing results. One particular unstructured tree was run 25 times in order to establish estimation error. The results of these runs are given in Figure 7.35.

Further features could confuse the timing figures. Some of the runs included checks for rule accuracy. This entailed a database lookup for every position. All the runs included a legal-move generator so that all legal positions could be tested. To determine how much of an overhead these two features entailed, 50 tree timing runs were performed with a null decision tree as the function to be evaluated and database checking turned off. A further 13 runs of the same null function were performed with database checking turned on. The results are shown in Figures 7.36 and 7.37.

	Time to classify all legal (209 718) positions (seconds)
Mean	35 315.85
Standard deviation	348.58

Figure 7.35 System timing tests using an unstructured decision rule. The same unstructured decision rule was run 25 times over all the legal KPa7KR WTM positions. Note the small standard deviation which shows that system load fluctuations do not play a significant role in timing results.

It would appear from these results that database lookup does not add to the user-execute time associated with a UNIX process.

Combining the above legal-move generation timing results and multiplying by the fraction of a kilobyte that is taken up by a null decision

Time to generate 209 718 legal positions database checks off (seconds)	
Mean	21 094.95
Standard deviation	300.66

Figure 7.36 Timing results for 50 legal-position generation runs. These figures will be used to establish the non-rule-related overhead of the previous timing runs.

Time to generate 209 718 legal positions database checks on (seconds)	
Mean	20 830.82
Standard deviation	397.44

Figure 7.37 Timing results for 13 legal-position generation runs. These figures will be used to establish the database lookup related overhead of previous timing runs.

Cost of generating 209 718 legal positions (kbs)	
Mean	731.8
Standard deviation	27.2

Figure 7.38 Timing results for the 63 null-function runs. These figures will be used as the non-rule-related overhead associated with classifying all the legal KPa7KR positions.

rule gives the figures shown in Figure 7.38. If this non-rule-related overhead is subtracted from the above sets of figures and the result divided by the number of legal KPa7KR WTM positions figures shown in Figure 7.39 are obtained.

For the KPa7KR WTM experiment the unstructured trees were on average 15.5% cheaper to run than the structured tree. This may be thought a small price to pay for human understandability.

Recall that during the development phase of the structured hierarchy four stages were saved for later evaluation against the classification database. The results are shown in Figure 7.40.

	Cost of classifying one position (kbs)	Approximate standard deviation
Structured tree	0.135	0.003
Unstructured tree	0.114	0.12

Figure 7.39 Mean classification cost of a KPa7KR WTM position. The standard deviation is approximate because the standard deviation of the overhead has not been taken into account (0.000 13 in all).

Stage no.	No. of new examples	Total examples so far	Positions wrong out of 209 718
1	101	101	1918
2	80	181	227
3	80	261	69
4	103	364	15

Figure 7.40 Accuracy of rule development stages. Stage 1 (initial top-down decomposition plus shallow training) was completed in the USA with about four man-weeks of effort. Stages 2 to 4 (further training by Danny Kopec and refinement) were completed in a further six man-weeks. The database only became available *after* the completion of stage 4. Using self-commenting as a diagnostic aid all 15 errors present after stage 4 were corrected in under two hours.

7.17 Programmer costs

Excluding the time taken to develop the tools to generate and test the structured rules, stage 1 (initial top-down decomposition plus shallow training) took four man-weeks to complete, stages 2–4 (further training by US National Master Kopec and refinement) took a further six man-weeks. It is interesting to note that the structured rule was 99.085% correct after four man-weeks but to find and correct the remaining 0.915% of the errors took a further six man-weeks. Skill in the new 'structured induction' style of program construction evidently accumulates and to some degree can be systematized with experience. The author was able, after the above work was completed, to instruct Mr Robert Reinke, a graduate student at the University of Illinois, in the methods, with the result that his continuation of this work to determine WFB/not WFB took less than two man-weeks (Shapiro, 1983, Appendix C). As shown in his report his experience with D. Fraisl on the WFW/not WFW for pb7 was fully confirmatory.

Chapter 8

Discussion

8.1 Database as oracle *versus* expert as oracle

Of the two modes of induction (structured and unstructured) investigated in this book, unstructured induction of either chess endgame would have been very difficult without a database to supply decision classes for attribute vectors. Likewise, without the availability of a domain expert to partition the problem space and supply relevant training examples, the structured approach would also have been very difficult. It follows that the non-availability of one or other of these resources (i.e. database or domain expert) largely predetermines the inductive mode that can be applied. Because of the initial non-availability of a KPa7KR database an unstructured approach was not possible until later when a database had been generated.

Oracle \ Mode	Unstructured	Structured
Database	poor	good
Expert	—	excellent

Figure 8.1 The effectiveness of computer induction. Ranked scores for 'brain compatibility' of the products of four induction regimes. All but the square marked '—' have been tested in this research.

Given an attribute set there are four different ways that induction can be performed. The four-fold table of Figure 8.1 shows the two modes of induction (structured and unstructured) versus the two sources of classificatory information (database and expert). The result tabulated within this matrix is the performance of the product when measured against the criterion of brain compatibility. Three of the entries in this table are confirmed by work reported in this book. It is expected that the fourth (the product of induction generated using unstructured induction and an expert to supply examples) would be more brain compatible than that generated using unstructured induction and the database to supply examples. This prediction should be tested.

There are two distinct modes of use for an oracle within the induction cycle:

- induction oracle; and
- checking oracle.

Quinlan's ID3 uses the same oracle for rule induction and rule checking, i.e. the database of decision-vectors for both rule induction and to determine (by finding no exceptions to the current rule) whether rule induction is complete. Interactive ID3 also uses the same oracle for both rule induction and rule checking – the expert (with a possible final appeal to a database for 'clean-up' to perfect accuracy). The examples supplied to date are used to induce a rule and further examples supplied by the expert are used to check it.

Given that both database and expert are freely available it is tempting to use the expert to supply the structure decomposition and the database to supply an exhaustive set of examples for each subproblem (as in the case of the KPK experiment). The advantage of this approach is that incorrectly classified examples will not be introduced. Incorrectly classified expert-supplied examples were a major source of annoyance in stages 1 to 3 of the KPa7KR experiment. These examples were not too difficult to detect because they eventually clashed with other expert-supplied examples. However, there is no guarantee that this would be the case with other problems and for more complex problems the incidence of this nuisance can be expected to increase. However, there is an overriding disadvantage to the use of databases as induction oracles, namely as concerns the human-like quality, or lack of it, in the generated rule. The KPK subtrees though linear are not as understandable as those generated for KPa7KR. One reason for this could be that since in KPa7KR we had no access to a classification database and thus no access to an exhaustive and correct source of decision-vectors, each attribute had to be developed with the expert in mind. Each attribute had to follow his specifications as closely as possible since he would in the end have to advise on any failing in their classificatory power. This was not the case with the attributes generated for the KPK subproblems. These attributes could be (and often were) altered to correct single failures to classify correctly. The resulting attributes were cumbersome and internally opaque. The alternative, as shown in the KPa7KR experiment, was that extra attributes should have been designed and possibly new subproblems introduced.

8.2 Meta-knowledge (old wives' tales and rules of thumb)

The need for some kind of expert guidance in the way the rules are formed first came to light while debugging the top-level subproblem pa7. Although a checkmate attribute was supplied, two of the examples in which White was checkmated:

1. WK:a8 WP:a7 BK:c7 BR:h8 and
2. WK:a1 WP:a7 BK:a3 BR:h1

were correctly classified as not WFW by other attributes (the first by wka8d and the second by wkchk). At first this was not disturbing to the experts because they do not immediately look for such rare occurrences as checkmate when classifying an endgame of this complexity. However, if all the advantages of self-commenting are to be utilized it is vital that positions are classified for the correct reasons. This problem could be overcome if a facility existed in Interactive ID3 for the expert to suggest a list of constraints that the rule being generated must obey, for example:

- chkmt must appear in the rule;
- bxqsq must always be followed by dq;
- chkmt if used must be followed immediately by stlmt;
- ds if used may only appear last in a rule.

Guidelines like those shown above are known as 'meta-rules'. They contain information not explicitly stated in the examples or the decomposition structure supplied by the expert. These meta-rules are information gathered by the expert in the form of rules of thumb accumulated from experience. Interactive ID3 should build a solution satisfying as many of these rules as possible. The application of such meta-rules has been manually simulated with success in a school algebra domain (Paterson, 1984).

Meta-rules are also useful for implementing efficiency considerations; recall the following table from Chapter 7.

Run-time behaviour for each test		
Test	Number decided	Leaving
thrmt	821 (TRUE)	187 506 undecided
wka8d	3 152 (TRUE)	184 354 undecided
wkchk	32 698 (TRUE)	151 656 undecided
dblat	6 962 (TRUE)	144 694 undecided
hdchk	30 (TRUE)	144 664 (FALSE)

Figure 7.11 dq decision tree (from Chapter 7).

Within a *linear* decision tree it is possible to permute the order of sequential tests that make identical decision discriminations. Another, functionally equivalent, order for this decision tree is shown in Figure 8.2. Note the order of tests allows the fastest filtering of positions through the rule.

```
wkchk
  f: dblat
    f: wka8d
      f: thrmt
        f: hdchk
          f: FALSE
          t: TRUE
        t: TRUE
      t: TRUE
    t: TRUE
  t: TRUE
```

Figure 8.2 Execution optimized dq decision rule. Assuming a random set of input positions this rule will be more efficient at run-time than the rule induced by Interactive ID3.

Another factor that can be taken into account when building a rule is the execution cost of tests. Some tests will be more resource expensive than others to run. Such information could be included with the set of meta-rules and applied by Interactive ID3 in combination with position filtering information like that shown in Figure 7.11.

A learning system that makes use of this kind of meta-knowledge in the form of rule templates is being developed at MIRU (Niblett, 1983).

8.3 Structured induction *versus* unstructured induction

The type of classification source available (i.e. either database or domain expert) influences the choice of mode of induction (structured or unstructured) to be applied. There is also the question of whether for sufficiently complex problems an unstructured solution could or should even be attempted. In both of the experimental chess domains, structured solutions were attempted first. Once these had been successful, complete and correct unstructured solutions were guaranteed by making use of the primitive attributes which were by now known to be able to discriminate between *all* legal positions in the problem domains. The author does not know how he would have attempted unstructured solutions without the benefit of this previous structured work. Without the prior structured pass over the problem, there would seem little hope of developing a set of attributes adequate for a complete solution of any kind. We thus arrive at the following conclusion:

> *A complex problem first needs to be tackled by the structured technique. But when it has yielded, no practical motivation remains for reworking it in unstructured mode. The evidence is that the product will disqualify itself on brain compatibility while failing to offer compensating advantages of run-time efficiency.*

8.3.1 QUALITY OF TRAINING EXAMPLES

There is a striking difference between the examples left in Quinlan's ID3 'working-set' following the generation of an unstructured rule compared to the examples left by Interactive ID3 following the generation of a structured rule. The examples left by ID3 after an unstructured run comprise a larger number altogether but far fewer examples that are meaningful to an expert. This is undoubtedly due to the experts' ability to supply meaningful examples and ID3's ability to filter still further and remove examples that do not contain unique features. The experts occasionally supplied redundant (sometimes duplicate) examples but all the examples were directed towards a preconceived solution framework. On the other hand in unstructured mode ID3, without any guidance, picked examples statistically and the resulting incomprehensibility of its rule reflected the arbitrariness of these examples. Could unstructured rule generation benefit from the use of the structured rule training set?

The answer to this question is found in the results section of Chapter 7 which shows that these 61 examples, though sufficient to produce a correct structured solution, were not sufficient to produce a correct unstructured solution. Thus supplying a structure actually increases the usefulness of a given set of relevant examples to an induction system. Put another way it could be said that the expert-supplied structure contains information. Section 8.3.2 seeks to place this statement on a quantitative basis.

8.3.2 INFORMATION CONTENT OF EXPERT-SUPPLIED STRUCTURE

By a slight extension of finite-message information theory (Michie, 1982a), entropy measures were calculated. We follow Attneave (1959) in using 'entropy' and the technical denotation of 'information' interchangeably.

1. *Entropy per symbol without classification rule* We construct a message using an **alphabet of two symbols**, {w, n} (WFW, not

WFW), by sampling M times from a set of 209 718 objects (KPa7KR WTM positions) each of which is labelled with one or other of the two symbols in the proportions P_w and P_n respectively. Sampling is with replacement and the final message has length M. The message is conceived as emanating from a **source** and being absorbed by a **receiver**. The receipt of each symbol incrementally conveys some information to the latter. The entropy per symbol is

$$-(P_w \times \log_2(P_w) + P_n \times \log_2(P_n))$$

where:

P_w is the frequency already known to the receiver of w objects in the set, here equal to the prediction probability of 'the next symbol is a w'.

$P_n = (1 - P_w)$.

We depart from the classical treatment by allowing the receiver to be at given points in time in different **knowledge-states**. We further distinguish **static** and **dynamic** receivers. A static receiver may change its state between messages but not from symbol to symbol during the receipt of a given message. A dynamic receiver may change its state in the light of information contained not only in past messages but also in the symbols received to date of a message whose receipt is not yet finished. Let us, as a bare-bones illustration, consider the information-content of a static receiver's possession of the value of P_w.

Case 1: Static receiver – no knowledge of the value of P_w. By the principle of insufficient reason, P_w is set at ½. Evaluation of the previous formula gives 1 bit per symbol, i.e. M bits in the total message.

Case 2: Static receiver – knowledge that P_w = 129 825/209 718. Evaluation of the above formula gives 0.959 bits per symbol, i.e. $0.959 \times M$ bits in the total message.

The information contained in the specification of P_w is the difference between these two cases and is equal to 0.041 bits per symbol, i.e. $0.041 \times M$ bits for a given message.

So much for the information content of a piece of knowledge (change of receiver's knowledge-state) when this is simply a number. Now we shall consider the information content of a structure or rule.

2. *Entropy per symbol after filtering each object through a rule* Objects that have been classified by a rule fall into four groups:

W_c – those objects that classify as w correctly: object is w, rule says w.

N_i – those objects that classify as w incorrectly: object is n, rule says w.

N_c – those objects that classify as n correctly: object is n, rule says n.

W_i – those objects that classify as n incorrectly: object is w, rule says n.

Figure 8.3 shows this more graphically. We now define the following probabilities:

P_w – described above but now specialized to the probability that an object picked at random is a w, equivalent to $(W_c + W_i)/(W_c + W_i + N_c + N_i)$. Note that since we are now dealing with a possibly faulty rule this quantity is no longer equal to the prediction probability.

P_n – As before this equals $(1 - P_w)$ which can now be described as $(N_c + N_i)/(W_c + W_i + N_c + N_i)$.

P_w^* – the probability that an object picked at random is classified as a w.

P_n^* – the probability that an object picked at random is classified as a n.

R_w – the conditional probability that if an object is w the rule says w. This is equivalent to $W_c/(W_c + W_i)$ (see Figure 8.3).

R_n – the conditional probability that if an object is n the rule says n. This is equivalent to $N_c/(N_c + N_i)$.

P_w' – the conditional probability that if the rule says w the object is w. This is equivalent to $W_c/(W_c + N_i)$.

P_n' – the conditional probability that if the rule says n the object is n. This is equivalent to $N_c/(N_c + W_i)$.

R_w and R_n can be thought of as measuring how 'representative' a rule is of an already known actuality. A general 'representivity' measure for a rule is as follows:

$$R = P_w \times R_w + P_n \times R_n$$

which means: the probability, for an object sampled at random, that the rule assigns it correctly to its class. Having defined these quantities Figure 8.3 is re-cast as a probability matrix in Figure 8.4.

Let us follow the same sequence of steps for P_w' and P_n' that we took with R_w and R_n. P_w' and P_n' can be thought of as measuring how 'predictive' a rule is of an actuality not yet known. A general 'predictivity' measure for a rule is:

$$P' = P_w^* \times P_w' + P_n^* \times P_n'$$

Note that working from Figure 8.3 we can quickly show that

$$R = P' = (W_c + N_c)/(W_c + W_i + N_i + N_c)$$

So a rule's representivity (which is an *a priori* way of looking at its reliability) is equal to its predictivity (which expresses the *a posteriori* view of its reliability).

Actual \ Rule	w	n
w	W_c	W_i
n	N_i	N_c

Figure 8.3 Confusion matrix for object classification through a two-valued decision tree.

Actual \ Rule	w	n
w	$R_w \times P_w$	$(1-R_w) \times P_w$
n	$(1-R_n) \times P_n$	$R_n \times P_n$

Figure 8.4 Probability matrix for object classification through a two-valued decision tree.

A **surprisal** (Samson, 1951) is derived from a **prediction probability** of a symbol as

$-\log_2(p)$, where p is the prediction probability.

In (1) above (knowledge of value of P_w, but no rule) there are two cases as follows:

Case α: object is w, surprisal $= -\log_2 P_w$

Case β: object is n, surprisal $= -\log_2 P_n$

The average surprisal per symbol is

$$P_w \times -\log_2 P_w + P_n \times -\log_2 P_n$$

which agrees with the entropy measure given in (1).

In (2) above (after the application of a rule) the symbols have surprisals as follows:

Case α: object is w.
Case A: rule says w, surprisal $= -\log_2 P'_w$
Case B: rule says n, surprisal $= -\log_2(1 - P'_n)$

Case β: object is n.
Case A: rule says w, surprisal $= -\log_2(1 - P'_w)$
Case B: rule says n, surprisal $= -\log_2 P'_n$

We need the average surprisal per symbol, as shown in Figure 8.5.

Case	Frequency	Term
αA	$R_w \times P_w$	$- R_w \times P_w \times \log_2 P'_w$
αB	$(1 - R_w) \times P_w$	$-(1 - R_w) \times P_w \times \log_2 (1 - P'_n)$
βA	$(1 - R_n) \times P_n$	$-(1 - R_n) \times P_n \times \log_2 (1 - P'_w)$
βB	$R_n \times P_n$	$- R_n \times P_n \times \log_2 P'_n$

Figure 8.5 Average surprisal per symbol as a sum of terms over four cases.

Item		Information (bits)
A	Initial information per symbol associated with the KPa7KR WTM chess endgame	0.959
B	Information per symbol associated with the structured solution and correct unstructured solutions	0.959
C	Mean information associated with the 66 unstructured decision trees trained with the structured training set	0.151
D	Standard deviation for above mean	0.109
E	Information associated with the *best* (most accurate) unstructured decision tree trained with the structured training set	0.410
F	Estimate of effective information per symbol associated with the structuring of the domain (by subtraction of *C* from *B*)	0.808

Figure 8.6 Information measures for the KPa7KR WTM problem and decomposition structure. *A* is the information per symbol associated with the KPa7KR WTM problem. *B* is the mean information per symbol associated with 66 decision rules that were generated without any expert-supplied structure but with the same examples that were sufficient to generate a complete and correct structured solution. The entropy associated with a correct decision rule is zero. So with the tools at hand, the loss of classificatory power and corresponding information are attributable to the removal of the expert-supplied structure.

Training set	Information per tutorial example (bits)
61 examples from the structured training set produced a rule with 0.151 bits of information per symbol.	0.002 5
An unstructured rule was generated using 175 examples. The rule classified perfectly, i.e. 0.959 bits of information per symbol.	0.005 5

Figure 8.7 Information per tutorial example.

The information gain (entropy difference) resulting from use of a 'knowledge-filter' is the average surprisal to a receiver in a state lacking the knowledge embedded in the filter *minus* the average surprisal to a receiver possessing the knowledge. The results obtained by the application of these formulae to the 66 unstructured trees generated using the structured training set are given in Figure 8.6. It should be noted that no effort has been made to take into account any difference in the efficiency of the ID3 induction algorithm when it is supplied with attribute sets of different sizes. In structured induction the algorithm only has to cope at any one time with a subset – namely those set aside as relevant to the given subproblem. Hence the failure of ID3 to generate more correct decision trees when structure is removed may be due in part to the nature of the ID3 induction algorithm. However, the results show that, using the available tools, the expert-supplied structure accounts for an estimated 84% of the classificatory power of the structured solutions. Since it has been shown that it is possible to generate a completely correct *unstructured* KPa7KR WTM decision rule using 175 examples, expert-supplied structure is equivalent to about 114 examples (structured induction required 61 examples, unstructured 175, and the difference is 114). The information per tutorial example in the two cases is given in Figure 8.7. These results show that the ID3 algorithm does a good job of extracting examples relevant to the rule being formed. Unfortunately, in the case of the unstructured rule, these examples are not necessarily meaningful to an expert. An experiment that would show the degree of relevancy these 175 examples have to the structured rule (and therefore perhaps to an expert) would attempt to reconstruct the structured rule using these 175 examples.

8.3.3 FURTHER CLASSIFICATION – DATABASE COMPRESSION

Recall in Chapter 2 when database compression was being discussed the following table was printed:

Domain	Database size (space of legal positions)	Number of decision vectors classifying the total space	Size of training set required to induce a complete and correct unstructured classification rule
KPK	83 622	2412	304
KPa7KR	209 718	3196	175

The same table is reproduced in Figure 8.8 showing the size of the training set required to induce a complete and correct rule by structured induction.

Domain	Database size (space of legal positions)	Number of decision vectors classifying the total space	Size of training set required to induce a complete and correct structured classification rule
KPK	83 622	2412	60
KPa7KR	209 718	3196	61

Figure 8.8 Further training-set reductions.

As before, these examples (together with formal definitions of the attributes and induction system) form a complete replacement for the original classification database in the sense that the latter can be reconstructed on the machine from the former. They also represent a powerful set of tutorial examples to explain *most* of the features of the structured rules (they may not explain features like attribute ordering which can sometimes be immaterial).

8.3.4 HUMAN UNDERSTANDABILITY OF RULES

The most important result to come out of this work is the discovery of the enhanced human understandability of rules generated by structured induction. This greatly increases the usefulness of induction in expert systems which (by definition) demand that users should be able to question the machine's rationale. There are two major questions that an expert system must be able to answer at run-time. These are:

1. How did the system arrive at this conclusion?
2. Why did the system ask this question or otherwise seek to evaluate this attribute?

Humanly intelligible rules coupled with the self-commenting explanatory feature make it possible to answer the 'How?' question while the condensed form of postfix self-commenting (described in Chapter 4) with slight changes (for future tense) provides an answer to the 'Why?' question. As an example of an answer to a 'Why?' question, imagine that the attribute values to the KPa7KR problem are obtained by questioning the user (and not by programmed attribute evaluation) and that the user has just been asked 'Is the BK attacked in some way by the promoted WP?'. If the user responded with 'Why?' the system response could be as shown in Figure 8.9.

---

if the BK controls the intersect point
    and the BK is not attacked in some way by the promoted WP
    seeing that the BK is not in the way
    and the WK is on an edge and not on a8
it will follow that there is a good delay because of a double attack threat
    and that there is a simple delay to white's queening the pawn
    and that this position is not won for white

Figure 8.9 Proposed form of answer to the 'Why?' question. System response after the user responds 'Why?' to the question 'Is the BK attacked in some way by the promoted WP'.

8.4 Nature of rule languages for computer induction

In Chapter 1 the need was indicated for constraints to be developed that would keep the products of induction within the bounds of brain compatibility. Working from the results of these experiments, which show that the human 'brain machine' when looked at as a computer can process decision trees providing that they are both linear and no more than about seven tests in length, a new type of computer language has been specified. CDL–1 (Concept Description Language 1; Michie, 1982b, 1983) accepts and processes all, and only those, expressions that are 'concept expressions'. The form of such expressions, based on findings with structured induction such as those reported in this book, is intended to ensure that they can be both understood and mentally applied. A program that generates only valid expressions of the CDL–1 language has been developed in PROLOG by Dr Ivan Bratko (visiting from the Josef Stefan Institute, Yugoslavia) together with an interpreter that executes these expressions. Appendix E shows the syntax of CDL–1 as implemented by my colleague Mr Steven Muggleton in the form of a compiler written in C.

8.5 Conclusions

Recall the question posed in Chapter 1 namely:

> *Can techniques for the use of induction be developed which, for the complex domain of KPa7KR WTM, make possible the generation of a complete and correct rule of solution which is both machine executable and brain compatible. When translated into English text can such a rule constitute a training aid?*

No such training aid exists for the domain in question whether humanly or semi-automatically generated. Moreover, no humanly generated training aid exists for any domain of comparable complexity in chess: this work in part has sought to shed light on the conjecture that at this level of task complexity the required codification is beyond unaided human power, but not beyond human power given the use of the new inductive tools.

Use of structured induction with self-commenting for the purposes of knowledge gathering and refining for KPa7KR WTM has led to the machine-aided generation of a solution that is both completely correct and literally self-explanatory. The complete rule-base, produced by rearranging the self-commenting text and adding a few keywords, is presented in Appendix F. Plainly it could have value as both a training aid and an advice text. The techniques used are themselves not complicated and are easily transferable to other workers in the field. Initially this text was produced by printing the expert-supplied attribute question-text in rule order and then rearranging and adding keywords by hand. Subsequently a computer program was written to perform this task and as a result errors were uncovered in the hand translation of the btoqs rule. The correct, machine-generated advice text for btoqs is appended to the hand-translated version presented in Appendix F.

8.6 Further directions

The work presented in this book has shown that using the techniques of structured induction and self-commenting, it is possible to extract from one or more experts knowledge that was previously inaccessible on a conscious level. The question now arises as to whether these techniques could be used to 'bootstrap' knowledge into an expert that previously was not available or even present in either man or machine. In other words could these techniques be used to aid experts on a course of investigation that would proceed not (as they do now) through introspection but through a guided man–machine partnership – each guiding the other through problem spaces that alone neither could penetrate?

This sort of investigation might proceed by the induction system proposing examples to the expert for validation. In the case of chess, the system could propose that the expert try and find positions that correspond to certain interesting attribute vectors not yet instantiated. As the search for these positions progresses other information may come to light that would indicate structural or attribute coding changes. If the system had better access to the primitive attributes it might be able to correlate their internal functionality and suggest which attributes might best be expanded to include others and which might best be split into further primitive attributes or possibly subproblems. The first step in this direction is being taken by my colleague Mr A. Paterson (1983) who is investigating the possibility of a clustering algorithm due to Michalski and Stepp (1982) supplying the hierarchical structure. This work is under the direction of Dr R. S. Michalski of the University of Illinois.

To a limited extent a process of 'knowledge creation' has already taken place. The author had no knowledge of the KPa7KR problem at the start of this work. Yet by the conclusion of stage 1 (before having contact with specialists in the field) a solution had been constructed that was accurate in all but 1% of the legal positions. This amount of knowledge was previously not available or present in any member of the stage-1 implementation team. Furthermore, throughout stages 2–4 the author found he was able to discuss the complexities of KPa7KR on an equal basis with US National Master Kopec (despite the fact that the author does not play chess). KPa7KR is still too simple a problem to exceed present human capabilities. A major question that needs answering concerns how well these techniques can function when the class values that an expert associates with situations are speculative or at best unverifiable.

To answer this question more development work must be done by way of languages and interactive environments for inductive systems. In order to perform this development work a suitably complex but well-defined problem will need to be found. The problem will need to be so complex that even the world's best experts disagree on classifications. Successful classification of the chess endgame KRPKR using the successors to the techniques presented in this book, would powerfully assist towards resolving the matter. We have been assured by A. J. Roycroft, one of the world's leading endgame scholars, that the KRPKR is not only beyond the articulacy horizon of the greatest experts but also far beyond their performance horizon in terms both of dependably correct classification and of choice of move.

References

Attneave, F. (1959). *Applications of information theory to psychology*. New York: Holt, Rinehart and Winston

Averbakh, Y. and Maizelis, I. (1974). *Pawn endings*. London: Batsford

Barrow, H. G. and Popplestone, R. J. (1971). 'Relational descriptions in picture processing' *Machine Intelligence 6*. Edinburgh: Edinburgh University Press, 377–396

Beal, D. (1977). 'K+P vs. K chess endgame – discriminating wins from draws' *Unpublished report*. London: Queen Mary College

Bitner, J. and Hansche, B. (1976). 'Topics concerning the KPK endgame' *Research report*, Urbana-Champaign: University of Illinois

Bramer, M. A. (1977). 'King and pawn against king: using effective distance' *Technical report*, March 1977, Milton Keynes: Open University

Chilausky, R., Jacobsen, B. and Michalski, R. S. (1976). 'An application of variable-valued logic to inductive learning of plant disease diagnostic rules' *Proceedings of the 6th Annual International Symposium on Multi-varied Logic*, Utah

Clarke, M. R. B. (1977). 'A quantitive study of king and pawn against king' *Advances in Computer Chess 1* (Ed. M. R. B. Clarke), Edinburgh: Edinburgh University Press, 108–118

Duff, M. J. B. (1978). 'Review of the CLIP image processing system' *National Computer Conference 1978*, 1011–1060

Feigenbaum, E. A. (1977). 'The art of artificial intelligence 1: themes and case studies of knowledge engineering' *STAN–CS–77–621*. Stanford: Department of Computer Science, Stanford University

Hunt, E. B., Marin, J. and Stone, P. (1966). *Experiments in induction*. New York: Academic Press

Kopec, D. (1982). 'Human and machine representations of knowledge' *Ph.D. Thesis*. Edinburgh: Machine Intelligence Research Unit

McKeon, R. (1947). *Introduction to Aristotle*. New York: Random House

Michalski, R. S. and Chilausky, R. L. (1980). 'Learning by being told and learning from examples: an experimental comparison of the two methods of knowledge acquisition in the context of developing an expert system for soybean disease diagnosis' *International Journal of Policy Analysis and Information Systems*, **4** (2)

Michalski, R. S. and Stepp, R. (1982). 'Revealing conceptual structure in data by inductive inference' *Machine Intelligence 10*. (Eds. J. E. Hayes, D. Michie and Y-H. Pao), Chichester: Horwood, 173–196

Michie, D. (1982). 'Computer chess and the humanisation of technology' *Nature*, **299**, September 1982, 391–394

Michie, D. (1982a). 'Measuring the knowledge-content of expert programs' *IMA Bulletin*, **18** (11/12), November/December 1982, 216–220

Michie, D. (1982b). 'Notes on CDL–1 for the output of APPRENTICE's rule-generator' *Internal Memorandum*. December 1982, Edinburgh: Intelligent Terminals Ltd

Michie, D. (1983). 'Allocation procedures: an extension to the CDL–1 language definition' *Internal Memorandum*. January 1983, Edinburgh: Intelligent Terminals Ltd

Michie, D. (1983a). 'Game playing programs and the conceptual interface' *Computer game playing*. (Ed. M. Bramer), Chichester: Horwood and New York: Halsted

Michie, D. and Chambers, R. A. (1968). 'BOXES as a model of pattern formation' *Towards a theoretical biology 1*, Edinburgh: Edinburgh University Press, 206–215

Michie, D. and Chambers, R. A. (1969). 'Man–machine co-operation on a learning task' *Computer graphics techniques and applications*. (Eds. R. D. Parslow, R. W. Prowse and R. Elliot Green), London: Plenum Press, 179–186

Newell, A., Shaw, J. C. and Simon, H. A. (1958). 'Chess-playing programs and the problem of complexity' *IBM J. Res. Dev.*, **2**, 320–335

Niblett, T. B. (1982). 'Validation of machine-oriented strategies in chess endgames' *Ph.D. Thesis*. Edinburgh: Machine Intelligence Research Unit

Niblett, T. B. (1983). 'An interactive rule induction system' *MIP–R–141*. Edinburgh: Machine Intelligence Research Unit

Nievergelt, J. (1977). 'The information content of a chess position, and its implications for the chess-specific knowledge of chess players' *SIGART Newsletter*, **62**, 13–15

Paterson, A. M. (1983). Personal communication

Paterson, A. M. (1984). 'Computer induction in a tutorial context' *M.Phil. Thesis*. Edinburgh: Machine Intelligence Research Unit

Quinlan, J. R. (1979). 'Discovering rules by induction from large collections of examples' *Expert systems in the micro-electronic age*. (Ed. D. Michie), Edinburgh: Edinburgh University Press, 168–201

Quinlan, J. R. (1983). 'Learning efficient classification procedures' *Machine learning; an artificial intelligence approach*. (Eds. R. S. Michalski, J. G. Carbonell and T. M. Mitchell), Palo Alto: Tioga, 463–482

Saavedra, F. (1895). Reported in *Practical chess endings*. (P. Keres 1974), London: Batsford, 89–90

Samson, E. W. (1951). 'Fundamental natural concepts of information theory' *Report E5079*. Air Force: Cambridge Research Station

Samuel, A. L. (1957). 'Some studies in machine learning using the game of checkers' *IBM J. Res. Dev.*, **3**, 210–229

Shapiro, A. (1983). 'The role of structured induction in expert systems' *Ph.D. Thesis*. Edinburgh: Machine Intelligence Research Unit

Shapiro, A. and Michie, D. (1986). 'A self-commenting facility for inductively synthesised endgame expertise' *Advances in Computer Chess 4*. (Ed. D. F. Beal), Oxford: Pergamon, 147–165

Shapiro, A. and Niblett, T. (1982). 'Automatic induction of classification rules for a chess endgame' *Advances in Computer Chess 3*. (Ed. M. R. B. Clarke), Oxford: Pergamon, 73–92

Voysey, H. (1977). 'Problems of mingling men and machines' *New Scientist*, **75** (1065), 18 Aug. 1977, 416–417

Winston (1970). 'Learning structural descriptions from examples' *Ph.D. Thesis (MAC TR–76)*. Massachusetts: Massachusetts Institute of Technology

Zdrahal, Z., Bratko, I. and Shapiro, A. (1981). 'Recognition of complex patterns using cellular arrays' *The Computer Journal*, **24** (3), 263–270

Zuidema, C. (1974). 'Chess, how to program the exceptions?' *Afdeling Informatica*, Amsterdam: Stichting Mathematisch Centrum.

Appendix A

An Unstructured KPK BTM WFW/not WFW Decision Tree

No. of examples in final working-set = 304.
No. of nodes in final tree = 79.
Time taken to generate rule = 243 CPU second.

```
imcap
  f: psquare
    f: wkahd
      f: LOST
      t: nearc8
        f: LOST
        t: DRAWN
    t: rookpawn_relevant
      f: pmove
        f: mp1
          f: r6patt
            f: dirop56
              f: mp56
                f: btop1
                  f: rank56_relevant
                    f: DRAWN
                    t: LOST
                  t: interfere
                    f: plus2
                      f: ahead
                        f: LOST
                        t: DRAWN
                      t: DRAWN
                    t: ahead
                      f: DRAWN
                      t: LOST
                t: rank56_relevant
                  f: rank7_relevant
                    f: mp2
                      f: diropw
                        f: interfere
                          f: DRAWN
                          t: LOST
                        t: LOST
                      t: LOST
```

```
                  t: stlmt
                    f: plus1
                      f: LOST
                      t: diropb
                        f: DRAWN
                        t: LOST
                    t: DRAWN
                t: LOST
            t: LOST
          t: LOST
        t: stlmt
          f: LOST
          t: DRAWN
      t: stlmt
        f: LOST
        t: mp1
          f: DRAWN
          t: LOST
    t: nearc8
      f: rp1
        f: near2p
          f: stalemate
            f: nearp
              f: rp2
                f: neara8
                  f: LOST
                  t: DRAWN
                t: DRAWN
              t: ahead
                f: plus2
                  f: LOST
                  t: DRAWN
                t: DRAWN
            t: DRAWN
          t: DRAWN
        t: LOST
      t: crit
        f: DRAWN
        t: plus1
          f: wkahd
            f: LOST
            t: DRAWN
          t: DRAWN
t: DRAWN
```

Appendix B

List of Chess Books Consulted by the Author for KPa7KR

Ban, J. (1972). *Tactics in the endgame*. Budapest: Athenæum

Barden, L. (1975). *How to play the endgame in chess*. New York: Bobbs-Merrill Co. Ltd

Fine, R. (1969). *Basic chess endings*. New York: McKay

Keres, P. (1974). *Practical chess endings*. London: Batsford, 89–93

Levenfish, G. and Smyslov, V. (1971). *Rook endings*. London: Batsford

Appendix C

Listing of btoqs Prior to its Being Made into a Subproblem

```
btoqs() { /* should really be a sub problem */
  if(bf < 3 && bf == wf && bf == rf && br > rr && rr > wr)
    return(comment(TRUE, FALSE, "", "", "", LEVEL));
  if(br > 6 && br == wr && br == rr && bf < rf && rf < wf)
    return(comment(TRUE, FALSE, "", "", "", LEVEL));
  if(wf == 2 && rf == 2 && ((wr > 4 && rr < wr)||
            (wr > 2 && rr > wr + 1 && !bitset(1, rr, BKING))) &&
               !(br+bf == 9 || br == 8))
    return(comment(TRUE, "YES because W can't avoid being skewered", "",
                          "", "", LEVEL));
  if(bf == 1) {
    if(br == 5 && rr == 1 && rf == 1 && wr == 1 && wf == 3)
      return(comment(TRUE, FALSE, "", "", "", LEVEL));
    if(rf == bf && rr < br && !(rr == 1 && wr == rr && wf == 3 && br != 3))
      if(!bitset(bf+2, br, WATT))
        return(comment(TRUE, FALSE, "", "", "", LEVEL));
      if(bitset(1, 4, ROOK) && bitset(1, 5, BKING) && wr == 4 && (wf == 3 || wf
                        == 4))
        return(comment(FALSE,
            "NO because the WK can keep the BK between the BR and WP",
            "", "", "", LEVEL));
    if(rf == 2 && rr < = br) {
    if(wr > br && wf == rf)
        return(comment(TRUE, FALSE, "", "", "", LEVEL));
      if((wf == 2 && wr < rr-2) || br <= 2)
        return(comment(TRUE, FALSE, "", "", "", LEVEL));
  }
    if(rf == 2 && bf < 3 && br < wr)
      return(comment(TRUE, "YES the BK aids the BR to skewer", "", "", "",
                          LEVEL));
    if(rf == 1) {
      expand(PAWN, 20);
      and(BATT, 20, 21);
      if(!zero(21))
        return(comment(TRUE, "YES the BK can sneak up on the WP", "", "", "",
                          LEVEL));
    }
  }
```

```
else if(br == 8) {
  if(bf == 3 && rf == 8 && rr == 8 && wf == 8 && wr == 6)
    return(comment(TRUE, FALSE, "", "", "", LEVEL));
  if(rr == br && rf > bf && !(rf == 8 && wf == rf && wr == 6 && bf != 6))
    if(!bitset(bf, br-2, WATT))
      return(comment(TRUE, FALSE, "", "", "", LEVEL));
  if(rr == 8) {
    expand(PAWN, 20);
    and(BATT, 20, 21);
    if(!zero(21))
    return(comment(TRUE, "YES the BK can sneak up on the WP", "", "", "",
                              LEVEL));
  }
}
cand(RATT, WATT, 21);
cand(PAWN, 21, 21);
cand(BATT, 21, 21);

/* WK in check and rook on edge with BK blocking posns */

  if(bitset(2, 7, 21)) {
    init(30);
    setbit(2, 7, 30);
    expand(30, 31);
    cand(31, DQ_INTERSECT, 31);
    if(zero(31))
      return(comment(FALSE, "NO because the BK is in the BR's way", "", "", "",
        LEVEL));
  }
  expand(21, 21);
  cand(BATT, 21, 21);
  and(DQ_INTERSECT, 21, 21);
  if(bitcount(21) == 2)
    return(comment(TRUE, "YES because the WK can't cover both BR intersect points",
                              "", "", "", LEVEL));
  return(comment(bitcount(DQ_INTERSECT) > bitcount(21), FALSE, "", "", "", LEVEL));
}
```

Appendix D

An Unstructured KPa7KR WTM WFW/not WFW Decision Tree

No. of examples in final working-set = 175.
No. of nodes in final tree = 82.
Time taken to generate rule = 963 CPU second.

```
rimmx
  f: bxqsq
    f: wknck
      f: bkxbq
        f: wkna8
          f: bkblk
            f: katri
              B: NOT
              W: WON
              N: wkpos
                f: reskr
                  f: wkcti
                    f: NOT
                    t: r2ar8
                      f: dsopp
                        f: thrsk
                          f: bkspr
                            f: skach
                              f: WON
                              t: NOT
                            t: NOT
                          t: NOT
                        t: WON
                      t: NOT
                  t: NOT
                t: rxmsq
                  f: wtoeg
                    1: dsopp
                      f: WON
                      t: dwipd
                        L: WON
                        G: skewr
                          f: WON
                          t: NOT
                    N: WON
```

```
                    t: qxmsq
                      f: NOT
                      t: WON
              t: hdchk
                f: spcop
                  f: rxmsq
                    f: WON
                    t: qxmsq
                      f: NOT
                      t: WON
                  t: NOT
                t: NOT
            t: bknwy
              f: NOT
              t: simpl
                f: r2ar8
                  f: WON
                  t: NOT
                t: NOT
          t: WON
        t: blxwp
          f: mulch
            f: bkona
              f: bkxcr
                f: wkovl
                  f: bkon8
                    f: bkxbq
                      f: thrsk
                        f: skach
                          f: skrxp
                            f: reskr
                              f: WON
                              t: NOT
                            t: NOT
                          t: NOT
                        t: NOT
                      t: WON
                    t: NOT
                  t: bknwy
                    f: NOT
                    t: WON
                t: NOT
              t: NOT
            t: NOT
          t: NOT
    t: NOT
  t: WON
```

Appendix E
Syntax of CDL–1

Nomenclature:

1. All upper-case words denote non-terminal symbols.
2. All lower-case words denote terminal symbols.
3. The construct [X|Y] means either X or Y.
4. The construct [X]+ means that X may occur one or more times.
5. The construct [X]* means that X may occur zero or more times.
6. The symbol –› means 'is defined as'.
7. A space means 'followed by'. Thus PROGRAM –› primitive [DEC]* PART[PROC]* means PROGRAM is defined as; primitive followed by zero or more DECs followed by PART followed by zero or more PROCs.

Note that anything in capitals can have its definition looked up in some lower line. Thus DEC in the definition of PROGRAM is itself defined on the following three lines. A construction like:

```
X  –›  a
X  –›  b
```

means X is defined as a *or* b.

Productions:

```
PROGRAM       –›   primitive [DEC]* PART [PROC]*
DEC           –›   int   DECLIST
DEC           –›   test  DECLIST
DEC           –›   NAME has cases { CASELIST }
DECLIST       –›   NAME [DECLREST]+
DECLREST      –›   , DECLIST
CASELIST      –›   NAME [CASELREST]+
CASELREST     –›   , CASELIST
PART          –›   to partition NAME P_COND_LIST OTHER_COND
PROC          –›   to decide NAME COND_LIST OTHER_COND
P_COND_LIST   –›   [P_COND]+
P_COND        –›   if PRED then CLASS
P_COND        –›   P_CASE_STAT
```

```
COND_LIST       ->   [COND]+
COND            ->   if PRED then CLASS
COND            ->   CASE_STAT
P_CASE_STAT     ->   in case NAME is P_CASE_REST
P_CASE_REST     ->   P_LOG_CASE
P_CASE_REST     ->   P_NUM_CASE
P_LOG_CASE      ->   PRED then TERM [P_NUM_C_TEST]*
P_LOG_C_CASE    ->   or if PRED then TERM
P_NUM_CASE      ->   < NUMBER then TERM [P_NUM_C_TEST]*
P_NUM_C_TEST    ->   or if < NUMBER then TERM
CASE_STAT       ->   in case NAME is CASE_REST
CASE_REST       ->   LOG_CASE
CASE_REST       ->   NUM_CASE
LOG_CASE        ->   PRED then TERM [LOG_C_TEST]*
LOG_C_TEST      ->   or if PRED then TERM
NUM_CASE        ->   < NUMBER then TERM [NUM_C_TEST]*
NUM_C_TEST      ->   or if < NUMBER then TERM
OTHER_COND      ->   otherwise CLASS
TERM            ->   CLASS
TERM            ->   if PRED then CLASS
PRED            ->   NAME
PRED            ->   not NAME
CLASS           ->   NAME
NAME            ->   ALPHA [ALPHANUM]*
ALPHANUM        ->   ALPHA
ALPHANUM        ->   NUMBER
ALPHANUM        ->   —
ALPHA           ->   [a|b|c|d|e|f|g|h|i|j|k|l|m|n|o|p|q|r|s|t|u|v|w|x|y|z]
ALPHA           ->   [A|B|C|D|E|F|G|H|I|J|K|L|M|N|O|P|Q|R|S|T|U|V|W|X|Y|Z]
NUMBER          ->   -[NUM]+
NUMBER          ->   [NUM]+
NUM             ->   [0|1|2|3|4|5|6|7|8|9]
```

Appendix F

WFW/not WFW Advice Text for KPa7KR WTM

The text which follows can be regarded as a fairly faithful free-hand translation of the C program generated by use of the structured induction interactive ID3 algorithm in the manner described in the body of this book. Conjunctions or disjunctions are chosen so as to minimize the number of negations while preserving meaning. The names of subproblems are capitalized for ease of identification. The numbers denote subproblem level as described in Chapter 7. As mentioned in Chapter 8, the rules for text manipulation were formalized in a program which when run showed the hand translation of the BTOQS rule to be in error. The correct BTOQS is appended to the hand-translated version.

List of rules

PA7, top-level rule This rule is used to decide if a KPa7KR position with White-to-move is won-for-White or not.

KPa7KR is won for White (PA7, 1) IFF
  the BR can be captured safely (rimmx)
  OR none of the following is true:
  there is a simple delay to White's queening the pawn (DQ, 2.1)
  OR one or more Black pieces control the queening square (bxqsq)
  OR the WK is in stalemate (stlmt)
  OR there is a good delayed skewer threat (DS, 2.2)

DQ, level 2.1 This rule is used in the PA7 (top-level) rule to decide if Black can successfully delay White from queening its pawn.

There is a simple delay to White's queening the pawn (DQ, 2.1) IFF
  there is a good delay because there is a mate threat (THRMT, 3.1)
  OR there is a good delay because the WK is on square a8 (WKA8D, 3.2)
  OR there is a good delay because the WK is in check (WKCHK, 3.3)
  OR there is a good delay because of a double attack threat (DBLAT, 3.4)
  OR there is a good delay because there is a hidden check (hdchk)

DS, level 2.2 This rule is used in the PA7 (top-level) rule to decide if Black can force a double attack of type 'skewer'.

There is a good delayed skewer threat (DS, 2.2) IFF
  there is a special opposition pattern present (spcop)

OR all of the following are true:

the WK is one away from the relevant edge (wtoeg)
AND the kings are in normal opposition (dsopp)
AND the WK distance to intersect point is too great (dwipd)
AND there is a potential skewer as opposed to fork (skewr)
AND the BK is not attacked in some way by the promoted WP (bkxbq)

THRMT, level 3.1 This rule is used in the DQ (level 2.1) rule to decide if Black can successfully delay White from queening its pawn because of an initial checkmate threat.

There is a good delay because there is a mate threat (THRMT, 3.1) IFF
the BR attacks a mating square safely (rxmsq)

AND

EITHER the BK can attack the WP (bkxwp)

OR none of the following is true:

the BK is attacked in some way by the promoted WP (bkxbq)
OR the mating square is attacked in some way by the promoted WP (qxmsq)
OR the BR does not have safe access to file A or rank 8 (r2ar8)

WKA8D, level 3.2 This rule is used in the DQ (level 2.1) rule to decide if Black can successfully delay White from queening its pawn because the white king is initially on the pawn promotion square (a8).

There is a good delay because the WK is on square a8 (WKA8D, 3.2) IFF
the WK is on square a8 (wkna8)

AND any of the following is true:

the BR has safe access to file A or rank 8 (r2ar8)
OR B attacks the WP (BR in direction x = −1 only) (blxwp)
OR a very simple pattern applies (simpl)

WKCHK, level 3.3 This rule is used in the DQ (level 2.1) rule to decide if Black can successfully delay White from queening its pawn because the white king is initially in check.

There is a good delay because the WK is in check (WKCHK, 3.3) IFF
the WK is in check (wknck)
AND the BR cannot be captured safely (rimmx)

AND any of the following is true:

B can attack the queening square soon (BTOQS, 4.2)
OR the BK can attack the critical square (b7) (bkxcr)
OR the BR bears on the WP (direction x = −1 only) (rkxwp)
OR there is a skewer threat lurking (thrsk)
OR B can renew the check to good advantage (mulch)

DBLAT, level 3.4 This rule is used in the DQ (level 2.1) rule to decide if Black can successfully delay White from queening its pawn because of an initial double-attack threat.

There is a good delay because of a double attack threat (DBLAT, 3.4) IFF
the WK is on an edge and not on a8 (cntxt)
AND the BK is not in the way (bkblk)
AND the BK is not attacked in some way by the promoted WP (bkxbq)

AND

EITHER the BK controls the intersect point (katri)

OR

the WK is in a potential skewer position (wkpos)
AND the potential double attack is good (OKSKR, 4.1)

OKSKR, level 4.1 This rule is used in the DBLAT (level 3.4) rule to decide if Black can successfully capitalize on a potential double-attack threat.

The potential double attack is good (OKSKR, 4.1) IFF
the BR has safe access to file A or rank 8 (r2ar8)
OR the WK cannot control the intersect point (wkcti)
OR the BK can support the BR (bkspr)
OR the BR alone can renew the skewer threat (reskr)
OR the WK can be skewered after one or more checks (skach)
OR the WK can be reskewered via a delayed skewer (reskd)

BTOQS, level 4.2 This rule is used in the WKCHK (level 3.3) rule to decide if any Black piece will soon be able to control the queening square as a result of the white king having initially been in check.

B can attack the queening square soon (BTOQS, 4.2) IFF
the BK is not in the BR's way (bknwy)
AND the BR can achieve a skewer or the BK attacks the WP (skrxp)
AND the BK is on file A in a position to aid the BR (bkona)
AND the BK is on rank 8 in a position to aid the BR (bkon8)
AND the WK is overloaded (wkovl)

Correct, machine-generated version of BTOQS, level 4.2:

B can attack the queening square soon (BTOQS level 4.2) IFF
the BK is not in the BR's way (bknwy)

AND any of the following is true

the BR can achieve a skewer or the BK attacks the WP (skrxp)
OR the BK is on file A in a position to aid the BR (bkona)
OR the BK is on rank 8 in a position to aid the BR (bkon8)
OR the WK is overloaded (wkovl)

List of unique primitives attributes invoked in the above text

- the BR can be captured safely (rimmx)
- one or more Black pieces control the queening square (bxqsq)

- there is a good delay because there is a hidden check (hdchk)
- there is a special opposition pattern present (spcop)
- the WK is one away from the relevant edge (wtoeg)
- the kings are in normal opposition (dsopp)
- the WK distance to intersect point is too great (dwipd)
- there is a potential skewer as opposed to fork (skewr)
- the BK is not attacked in some way by the promoted WP (bkxbq)
- the BR attacks a mating square safely (rxmsq)
- the BK can attack the WP (bkxwp)
- the mating square is attacked in some way by the promoted WP (qxmsq)
- the BR does not have safe access to file A or rank 8 (r2ar8)
- the WK is on square a8 (wkna8)
- B attacks the WP (BR in direction $x = -1$ only) (blxwp)
- a very simple pattern applies (simpl)
- the WK is in check (wknck)
- the BK can attack the critical square (b7) (bkxcr)
- the BR bears on the WP (direction $x = -1$ only) (rkxwp)
- there is a skewer threat lurking (thrsk)
- B can renew the check to good advantage (mulch)
- the WK is on an edge and not on a8 (cntxt)
- the BK is not in the way (bkblk)
- the BK controls the intersect point (katri)
- the WK is in a potential skewer position (wkpos)
- the WK cannot control the intersect point (wkcti)
- the BK can support the BR (bkspr)
- the BR alone can renew the skewer threat (reskr)
- the WK can be skewered after one or more checks (skach)
- the WK can be reskewered via a delayed skewer (reskd)
- the BK is not in the BR's way (bknwy)
- the BR can achieve a skewer or the BK attacks the WP (skrxp)
- the BK is on file A in a position to aid the BR (bkona)
- the BK is on rank 8 in a position to aid the BR (bkon8)
- the WK is overloaded (wkovl)

Index